Evandro Carlos Torezan

Cora and me

Adventures of a lone cyclist on the Way of Cora Coralina

1st edition

Brasília
Author's Edition
2021

Factsheet

Coordination and organization
Evandro Carlos Torezan

Cover photos
Evandro Carlos Torezan

Graphic design and cover
Evandro Carlos Torezan

Proofreading
Luísa Toresan Moreira da Silva

T681c Torezan, Evandro Carlos, 2021
Cora and me / Evandro Carlos Torezan. --
Brasília,DF: 2021
1st edition
132 p.

ISBN 978-65-00-17286-7

1. Way of Cora Coralina 2. Cycling trip 3. Personal narratives I. Evandro Torezan II. Title

CDD 918.1
CDU 82-94

To Grandma Santa,
that in 2019 completed
101 years old.

I

Introduction

Thirty days before, everything seemed settled. The vacation was booked, my cycling friends confirmed, the group was formed. It was time for another cycling trip. This time, the newly opened Way of Cora Coralina was the chosen route. However, as those thirty days passed... my companions gave up on accompanying me. One of them capitulated in the face of marital might. The other declared himself without financial resources. And now? Give up? The idea of cycling alone was not in my plans, but they began to change by chance of fate.

Annually, Sindilegis (Labor Union of the Brazilian Congress), to commemorate Public Labor's Day, invites some famous personality to speak to its members. When I heard that in 2018, Amyr Klink would be the speaker, I was thrilled. I have known Amyr since I was a teenager, by name, of course. I then rescued an old book written by Amyr, named *A hundred days between heaven and sea,* written in 1985, and began to read it. In the first chapters the idea of traveling alone began to take shape.

In the book, Amyr reports the adventure that made him famous. In a small wooden boat, the I.A.T., the navigator crossed the Atlantic Ocean, paddling from Africa to Brazil. Lonely on his boat, Klink had to be meticulous while planning the trip. Any miscalculation could be fatal. He had to think about a lot of things: food, hydration, boat design, communication, bureaucracy. All this in a time without the Internet. In his hundred days of isolation, he had fishes, whales and sharks as company. He guided himself like the old navigators, by the sun and by the stars, because the Global Positioning System (GPS) became operational only in 1995, more than ten years after his trip.

As I advanced in reading, I decided: I would cycle alone! Of course, the achievements are not comparable. Amyr's book just helped me decide, inspired me to try a new experience. If he crossed an entire ocean and arrived alive on the other side, why couldn't I pedal for about four hundred solitary kilometers through Goiás?

The planning evolved. I would start traveling on a Sunday, after the October 12th holiday, to avoid finding crowded hotels. I prepared my tracklogs carefully. I decided to start cycling from my house, stretching the route more than a hundred kilometers. I wasn't going to need to use the stars to guide me through Goiás lands because, in addition to Garmin GPS, I would also have my phone, which has GPS antenna, as a backup. Holy tech!

The bike preparation was special. On my bike trip along the Way of Santiago (Spain), in May 2018, I had problems with it. In the transport, the back rack broke. When I realized the problem, while riding my bike for the first time in the small French town of Saint Jean Pied de Port, I was worried: "How am I going to fix this here in France?" I'll explain: the frame I took, Scott Scale 960, is not prepared for installation of racks and I had to make adaptations. My friend Dalton Schneider used his blacksmith skills and adapted an old seatpost rack to my frame. The service was great and lasted the stride for four years. However, in emergencies like this, the Scott frame does not allow me to go to the nearest store and buy a new rack. I had to find a welder in France! Do you know how to say "weld" in French? Yeah, me neither, either in French or Spanish.

With this incident, I decided to change the frame and buy a reinforced rack when I returned to Brazil. After a lot of research and talks with fellow bicycle travelers, I acquired a First Atrix frame and a Topeak Explorer rack. Everything arrived in the mail a month before the trip. I had plenty of time to assemble, ride and test the new bike and rack.

Everything was ready. The only thing left was to leave.

II

Cora Coralina and the way

Cora Coralina

Ana Lins dos Guimarães Peixoto was born in 1889 in Villa Boa de Goyaz, now Cidade de Goiás (City of Goiás), the first State Capital. In her childhood, Ana studied two "books" (at the time, basic education was not divided into grades, but in books), learning to read, write and perform basic mathematical operations. At the age of fourteen she began writing poems and short stories under the pseudonym Cora Coralina, which means Red Heart, according to her.

She ran away from home at the age of 22, with divorced lawyer Cantídio Tolentino de Figueiredo Brêtas, going to live in São Paulo's inland (State of São Paulo, Brazil). In 1934, 45 years old, she became a widow. Then, she moved to the City of São Paulo, where she worked as a book seller to support her children. In 1956, she returned alone to the City of Goiás, because her children were all married. She went to live in the house where she was born, on the banks of the Vermelho River (Red River), in Goiás downtown. There, she devoted herself to the production of candy, a craft that, like writing, marked her life. In one of her verses, she declares, *"I am more of a confectioner and a cooker than I am a writer"*.

Her first published book was *Poema dos becos de Goiás e estórias mais (Poems of the alleys of Goiás and more stories)*, when she was over seventy years old. From then on, she gained notoriety, even occupying the chair number five of the Women's Academy of Letters and Arts of Goiás. In 1980, she received praises from Carlos Drummond de Andrade (famous Brazilian poet and writer) and became popular.

Ana died in Goiânia in 1985, at the age of 94.

Her poetry portrays her everyday life, her relationship with nature and with society. It depicts the day to day of the Goian people, the country man, the farmer, the cattle.

The Way of Cora Coralina

Contrary to what many people think, Cora Coralina did not walk the path that takes her name. It is only a tribute to the internationally renowned poet who is one of the greatest representatives of Goian culture. Her verses decorate the way. When less expected, in the middle of the forests, in the curves of the roads, on the banks of rivers, plaques appear with excerpts from Cora's poems.

The texts were taken from Cora's books, such as *Meu livro de cordel (My cordel book)*, *Vintém de Cobre (Copper Vintém)* and *Poemas dos becos de Goiás e estórias mais (Poems of the alleys of Goiás and more stories).* Whoever made the plaques, they did not have the care that Ana deserves. There are exchanged words, typos, commas, and dots not placed in the original places, uppercase letters exchanged for lowercase. I checked all the texts that were reproduced in this book and corrected the errors. However, I could not find the source of some of them, which I left as they were written on the plaques of the path.

The Way of Cora Coralina is a long-distance trail. It's a three hundred kilometers path through the State of Goiás. The path passes through historical cities, farms, public and private environmental conservation units. The route connects Corumbá de Goiás to Cidade de Goiás, popularly known as Goiás Velho (Old Goiás). It is not the smallest way between the cities. It was sought to make the best way, with more historical cities and more natural parks. To go through it, just follow the yellow footprints in which you read the stylized name "Cora". They are painted on trees, rocks, plaques, fences.

The path's project was developed by the State Agency of Tourism of Goiás (Goiás Turismo), but it was shelved for many years, in which some punctual actions were executed, such as the placement of signs, the definition of the course, the elaboration of executive project, but the route was forgotten and the few brave people who tried to go through it found a lot of abandoned stretches and little information. In 2018, Goiás Turismo took the project off the paper and materialized it. Nowadays, those who walk through it pass through beautiful waterfalls, take baths in crystal-clear water rivers, eat delicious homemade food, sleep in old farms, see the history preserved in old mansions, churches and historic buildings.

They are old paths, some existing since the 17th century, when the *bandeirantes* pioneered the lands of the Brazilian Midwest in search of riches. Some paths have already turned into paved roads, but the project tried, as much as possible, to follow dirt routes.

Although it is not a religious pilgrimage route, the path passes through several churches that can be visited.

The highlights of the Cora Way are:

- The poetry of Cora Coralina, found on plaques along the way;
- The Goian food that can be enjoyed in the cities;

- Historical cities like Pirenópolis, Corumbá de Goiás and Cidade de Goiás;
- Natural landscapes such as Salto Corumbá, Pireneus Park and Jaraguá Hills.

It's one of the best long-distance trails in Brazil. Go through it without haste.

III

Tips

Don't travel alone

It's hard to cycle or walk alone in a long-distance trail. I went alone, but I will probably not repeat the experiment. If a problem occurs, you will have no one to help! Even with mechanical knowledge, certain equipment breakdowns require more than two hands to be solved. In case of a serious accident, the rescue may not arrive in time. It's always better to have someone with you.

GPS is necessary

Do not travel without the tracklog loaded in a GPS. The path signs exist, but are not integral. There are faulty and confusing points, as well as stretches with breaches in the markings that will leave you in doubt.

Updated tracklog

Download the updated tracklog on *serpedalante.com/cora* . There, you will get the tracklog I recorded. The tracklog I took, downloaded from a website, had some holes that left me lost for a few minutes until I found my way again. I covered a hundred percent of the way and recorded the whole route. Download the tracklog and follow safe!

Beware of animals

It isn't wild animals that will bother you, the problem is the domestic ones. There is a lot of cattle. Carefully pass through the pastures and corrals. Do not scare them. Do not surprise them. Do not corner them. You must pass grouped. Cows with calves are dangerous, nervous, get away from them.

If a dog chases you, do not stop pedaling. Throw water on it with your bottle.

Food

The Goian food is great. It's easier to find restaurants open during the day. At night, there are street food options. Enjoy the steak skewers with set meal as much as you can. They are the urban gastronomy revolution. Simple and cheap meal, that contains barbecue and usually rice, beans, cassava and salad. It will provide you energy for the next day activities.

Path Sections

Day 0: **Brasília - Corumbá de Goiás** (distance: 118 km / climb: 1,749 m)

I called it day zero because this section is not part of the official Way of Cora Coralina, but for those who want to include two more historical cities in the way, or landed in Brasília, it is a viable option. It departs from Brasilia, passing through Santo Antônio do Descoberto and Olhos D'água (Waterhole Springs). Have a lunch in Olhos D'água. Then, it is almost just paved roads. There are also other ways to get to Corumbá, shorter ones, without going through Olhos D'água, but they're not the subject of this book.

Day 1: **Corumbá de Goiás - Pirenópolis** (distance: 55 km / climb: 1,125 m)

Despite the small distance, the route is time consuming. Enjoy each meter as it is the most beautiful section of the entire trip. Between Parque dos Pirineus and Pirenópolis there's a lot of singletracks, some parts have so many boulders that you cannot pedal, and others, in the middle of the forest, are confusing. Have lunch at Sombra da Mata Camping (the path passes inside it), which is located after the Parque dos Pireneus Highway. A few kilometers after the camping, you will enter the Gold Trail, which border the "das Almas" River and ends in downtown Pirenópolis. All the fences that you will have to jump that day, approximately ten, belong to this trail.

It's hard to pass alone if the bike is loaded. If you think you will be unable to jump the fences, follow the highway until the town. If you think you can do it, go through Gold Trail, because it is very interesting.

Day 2: **Pirenópolis - São Francisco de Goiás** (distance: 78 km / climb: 1,660 m)

It is a tiring section. The passage through the "das Pedras" River (Stones River) is complicated for those with a loaded bike. The cyclist will need to remove the baggage to cross a small dam. Caxambu Hills is a beautiful challenge, both to climb and to descend.

There are grocery stores in Caxambu, where you can grab a bite. Have lunch in Radiolândia, at Mercado Miranda. Order lunch in advance, especially if you're in a group. From Radiolândia to São Francisco, it is approximately 25 kilometers, with no great climbs.

Day 3: **São Francisco de Goiás - Jaraguá** (distance: 40 km / climb: 883 m)

Usually, on the third day, cyclists head to Itaguari. As the ascent of the Jaraguá Hills is gorgeous, I decided to go up unhurriedly and sleep in Jaraguá. From São Francisco to the beginning of the hills, the route accompanies the Jari River, so there is not much altimetric variation.

To climb the Jaraguá Hills you have three alternatives:

1st) Official path: it is two and a half hours in the middle of the bush and Brazilian Savanna (*cerrado*) with an hour pushing the bike uphill. The trail rises on the west side of the mountain, reaches the lookout point and descends to Jaraguá. It's a very difficult route, especially the uphill-push-bike, which has very steep sections. It's hard to go through it without help, but the landscape is worth the effort.

2nd) Inverted route: it is two hours in the middle of the bush/*cerrado* with thirty minutes of push-bike on the descent. Go straight to Jaraguá, up to the lookout point and then down the singletrack. The inverted ascent is fully pedalable, hard, but pedalable. Going down the singletrack will be difficult, but much easier than climbing, and you can enjoy the view.

3rd) Inverted route without singletrack: one hour in the middle of the bush/*cerrado*. Go straight to Jaraguá and then up to the lookout point. Go back through the same path. You will avoid the singletrack and save more than an hour, but will not lose the sight of the top of the Jaraguá Hills.

If you have time, stay overnight in Jaraguá. If you don't, have lunch and head to Itaguari. If you are going to stay overnight in Jaraguá, there's also the option to go straight to the city, leave the load at the hotel and return, making the climb with no weight.

Day 4: **Jaraguá - Itaguari** (distance: 50 km / climb: 895 m)

You will travel parts of the path you have been through the day before. When picking up the fork to Vila Aparecida, new sections begin to appear. Then, you will pass through other small villages like Alvelândia and Palestine. Sections with many farmings and pastures. Itaguari is a small town with only one lodging option.

Another viable option is to cycle to São Benedito and from there to Itaberaí, a larger city with more hotels and inns. On the next day, you will have to go back to São Benedito to continue the path.

Day 5: **Itaguari – Cidade de Goiás** (distance: 91 km / climb: 1,336 m)

In São Benedito, there is a bar on the side of the highway that crosses the village, where *tapiocas* are served, a good option for a snack or lunch. Just after São Benedito, when the path returns to the dirt road, there is a balneary, great place to rest. Have lunch in Calcilândia, in a bar at the entrance to the city where there are always trucks parked. The owner prepares lunch. If your group is large, it's best to order in advance. Be careful on the way out of Calcilândia so you don't get lost. There is a confusing sign indicating "Goiás." Take the narrow road on the left, which comes out of the widest. From there, the path becomes prettier, but harder, passing through areas of *cerrado* and isolated forests. After leaving this isolated area, you enter a pasture area with sections of forest where you need to be very careful to not get lost. When you reach the paved road, a few kilometers from City of Goiás, the original path used to enter a gate on the right to take the Estrada Real (Royal Road), however, the owner of the area closed the access and now it is necessary to follow the highway straight to the city.

IV

Day zero

Brasília, October 14, 2018.

***"Numa ânsia de vida eu abria o vôo nas asas impossíveis do sonho."* Cora Coralina**

"In a longing for life I opened the flight in the impossible wings of the dream." Cora Coralina

I was eager to go. Sometimes, we decide something that contradicts our convictions and this contradiction keeps turning our heads. What if the bike breaks? What if it rains so hard that pedaling becomes impossible? What if the night catches me on the trail, away from cities? What if I fall off a bridge, get hurt and hide in the river gutter? Despite having solutions to almost everything, I was tense and did not sleep very well.

But what would man become if he did not defy his fears? If he stayed home watching life go by? This curiosity is what drives humanity forward. The butterflies flying in our stomach before facing the unknown, the cotton mouth, the fear keeps us on alert and makes us prepared for what's coming. We must face our fears, not to overcome them, only to learn how to live with them.

Quarter to five a.m. Tense, but prepared, I left home for a different experience: cycle-traveling solitary through the inland Goiás. I took on my bike everything I needed to survive the week. That is a feeling I really like to feel, when I go around on my adventures. Living is simple, life requires very little, humans complicate everything.

On the way out of the condo, the doorman, seeing me taking the loaded bike, asked me jokingly: "Are you going to travel?" People still find it strange that someone who has a car travels, or goes to work, by bike. They think that a bicycle is a toy or something that only someone that cannot buy a car uses. In Brasília, a city that has many cyclists, this prejudice is softer, but exists. I said: "Yes, I am going to Goiás." Then he asked me if I was going to Entorno (region that borders the Brazilian Federal District). I explained to him that I was going to the City of Goiás and that it would take four to five days to reach my destination. He made a face of disbelief. Without lengthening the conversation, I left.

I pedaled to the Arniqueiras Subway Station, meeting point previously scheduled with my friend Silvio Sá. At least on the first day I would have company. He did not take long to get there.

We continued to climb the streets of Águas Claras and pass through Taguatinga before reaching BR-060 Highway. The first day of a cycling trip is to adapt to the weight of the luggage. The climbs get harder, the bike loses agility. We follow the road, passing through Samambaia, where the sun began to warm us up. After the junction of BR-060 with DF-180, we took a detour by dirt road that took us directly to the Água Quente Housing Sector, in DF-280, passing through the landless camps that exist in the area and crossing the Samambaia River twice. With 35 kilometers, we crossed the bridge over the Descoberto River, the Federal District western border, and reached Santo Antônio do Descoberto.

Santo Antônio do Descoberto

Santo Antônio, today "do Descoberto", was "dos Montes Claros". The hilly region between Ponte Alta (Gama) and Santo Antônio was known, in the *bandeirantes* times, as Montes Claros (Clear Hills). In 1722, the Bartolomeu Bueno da Silva's expedition, the Anhanguera-Son, set up camp in the place where the city was formed. With the discovery of gold in 1757, the entire surroundings of the city became an immense mine, becoming the third most important of the late Santa Luzia Judgment (present-day Luziânia).

There's almost nothing left of its historical buildings, only the church, which has interesting history. According to the legend, in the days of mining, two mining slaves found an image of Santo Antônio de Pádua next to an *angico* tree. The image was taken to the Santa Luzia Church, but miraculously disappeared from the church and reappeared in the *angico* tree where it was found. The fact was repeated several times: taken to church, disappeared and reappeared in Santo Antônio. The priest even kept the image inside a safe, but it didn't work, the miracle occurred in the same way. In 1770, the church was built, where the image was permanently transferred and from where it never disappeared. Over time, the building was being renovated and lost its original features.

- - -

We stopped at a bakery in town and had breakfast.

Santo Antônio was once the most violent area surrounding Federal District, so, crossing it is always tense. We crossed the city from east to west, following the road GO-225. I climbed the Descoberto River valley as if I was dragging a tram. What a weight! We left the paved road when we reached the dirt road that goes to the Areias River (Sands River), at 45 kilometers of pedal.

The dirt road crosses a plateau before it begins to descend the Areias valley. With 56 kilometers we got to the bridge of the extinct Vilmo's Bar. The river was full, with muddy waters, quite different from the last time I was there. Without delay, we started to go up. The slope after the bridge is a big challenge. Two hundred meters of ascent in six kilometers. At the top we had surprises: *mangaba* and cashew (*cajuí*) trees fruiting. We stopped to enjoy the fruits and rest. The good thing about cycling in October through *cerrado* is that you always find some native fruit.

We cycled a few kilometers up the top until we started to descend into the deep Valério's Stream. The road was good, no dust, but I went down carefully to avoid problems in the bike rack, and I climbed equally slow due to the cargo I was carrying. I think I have ever passed so slow through this area. How different it is! The speed changes everything. I could observe the stream, with clean waters, the riparian forest that accompanies the road for a few hundred meters before starting the eucalyptus forest that follows to the top of a plateau. It was 150 meters of ascent in 3.5 kilometers. We rested on the top, under the shade of a eucalyptus lane.

We went through the plateau. On the other side it is possible to see a great *buritizal* (*buriti* is a palm tree and *buritizal* is a wood of *buritis*) in the Muquém Stream, beautiful grove, but it is with its days numbered. Besides the dam the land owner made in the lower part, the entire surrounding *cerrado* was removed. The *cerrado* was replaced by plantations, irrigated by central pivots with the dam waters. Some of the *buritizal*'s arms are already dying.

Coming down the plateau, we found a *cagaita* tree on the side of the road. We made another stop to enjoy the fruit. *Cagaita* is a misleading fruit. If you eat a lot, loosens the intestines. That's where its name comes from: *cagar* in Portuguese means to shit. However, by one whim of Mother Nature, the solution is in the tree itself: drinking an infusion with your leaves ceases diarrhea.

We crossed the Muquém Stream and the Cachoeira Creek, with its challenging valleys. The climb of the Cachoeira, seen from afar, is frightening, but up close is not so bad. So, we get to road GO-139. We crossed it and took the road GO-561, through which we follow for two kilometers to the first curve. There we left the asphalt and took the old access of Olhos d'Água, a dirt road that goes directly to the village. From the top you can see the church, imposing in the middle of the houses. There is a huge gully by the side of the road. It is the cause they abandoned it. The bridge over the Galinhas Creek, by the way, was redone several times. The upper side, where we stepped, was lined with thin tree trunks a little spaced, looking like a cattle guard. I crossed carefully so I wouldn't fall. On the other side of the river is Olhos d'Água, where we entered around 11 o'clock. Entering the village by this dirt road is much more interesting than doing it by the paved road. There are some houses shaded by the riparian forest, humid and pleasant environment.

Olhos d'Água (Waterhole Springs)

Santo Antônio dos Olhos d'Água is not that old. It was founded when farmers donated lands to build a church. The first cross was erected in 1940. The community grew as rural residents began building houses around the church, becoming Corumbá de Goiás district in 1954. In 1960, with the announcement of the construction of Brasilia, the city suffered a severe blow. The city headquarters was transferred to the margin of BR-060 Highway, where Alexânia was formed.

Olhos d'Água was reborn with tourism. There are only a few natural attractions, such as the beautiful Rio do Ouro and some waterfalls, but the main attraction in the small village is the cultural tourism. There are beautiful colonial-styled houses around the church.

Twice a year, on the first weekends of June and December, the Exchange Fair takes place. Performed since 1974, at this fair it is possible to exchange products of all kinds, such as clothing, footwear, vinyl records, crafts in general, food, books. But, if you do not have anything to trade, you can buy.

\- - -

We headed straight to the Bar do Ciclista (Cyclist Bar), where we stopped to ease the thirst. We ate something and rested for about twenty minutes.

We return to pedal passing through quiet street, sand floor, many trees, houses of varied styles. When we went up a wider street, to get out of the village, Silvio's bike chain came loose and got tangled up in such a way that we could not undo it. Silvio had to take it apart. Repair done, we left town.

We took a dirt road that goes to the Botinha's Bar without going through the paved road. At first, it passes through a section of *cerradão* (Brazilian savanna with taller trees than common *cerrado*). When we left the bush, we saw that the weather was getting worse. The heat was great, it was stuffy and humid. We rode ten kilometers to get back to road GO-139.

When passing through the road fork, right where the Botinha's Bar is, we find a flock of rheas grazing in a newly harvested crop, a scene that has become increasingly rare with the constant suppression of *cerrado* and native fields in the State of Goiás. We contemplated the grazing of the birds for a few minutes.

It was 25 kilometers to go to Corumbá. We followed the road GO-225, highway that was recently paved. The section is difficult. There are three deep valleys in the rivers “do Ouro”, Retiro and Congonhas.

And their climbs are long, endless I would say. Riding a loaded bike, I suffered in all of them. The relief only came when we spotted Corumbá.

Corumbá de Goiás

Corumbá is a historical city. It was born at the age of *bandeiras* (literally "flags": Portuguese expeditions by South America in Imperial period), in 1731, on the beards of the mines of the Corumbá River and Bagagem Stream. The village was formed on the left bank of the river, but in 1733, after an attack by Indians, it migrated to the right bank. With the construction of the Nossa Senhora da Penha de França Chapel, Corumbá grew between it and the river.

With this physical limit (the river), the bridges always had great importance to the city. The narrow and historical wooden bridge built by engineer João José de Campos Curado (grandson), a member of the Cruls Mission, although ancient, remains very important for people. Its construction began in 1897 and ended in 1900. For seventy years it was the only link between the two sides of the city. During the construction of Brasilia, it endured the traffic of trucks that brought machinery, materials and workers to the new capital. Currently, in the urban perimeter there are only two bridges over the Corumbá River.

The city has preserved colonial houses and antique churches in its small old town. In addition to the architectural attraction, the city has beautiful waterfalls around it, among which stands out the famous Corumbá Falls.

- - -

At 2 p.m., we arrived in Corumbá de Goiás. We crossed the Corumbá River and stopped at the restaurant O Casarão, on the side of road BR-414, which crosses the city. I was very hungry. We had lunch there, no hurry.

After lunch, I went to find a place to spend the night. Without many options, I chose the clean and simple Gaúchos Inn, in front of the city bus station. Meanwhile, Silvio went to the bus station, bought his ticket back to Brasilia and left at 4 p.m.

From that moment on, I would be alone. Now, it was God and me on the Way of Cora Coralina. God, the poems of Cora Coralina and me.

I went to the hotel and did not leave until night fell, when I left looking for a restaurant.

Sunday night. The city was a desert. I walked through the dark, uneven, narrow, empty streets. There wasn't a soul to give information. I headed for the old town. I had seen a diner there and it could be open. No, it was not. I realized then that there was a crowd of people near the church. I went there. There was an amusement park in the city, set up on a wide street in downtown. All there was were toys stalls and candy. Oh my god! Do the people of this town not eat dinner out? I could not find anything, not even a hot dog shack.

I went back to the Casarão Restaurant. There were only snacks to eat. I asked the attendant to warm some up for me and sat at the tables on the balcony. At a table next to me, some young people were gathered. I could not help overhearing the conversation. Besides to listening songs that adhered to violence and drug use, they smoked stinking cigarettes. "I'd better get back to the hotel," I thought. I finished eating, ordered another snack to go, paid the bill and left. It's better, and safer, to sleep early.

Day zero completed, after all, the Cora Coralina Way begins in Corumbá de Goiás.

Summary of the day: 118 kilometers traveled with 1,749 meters of climb.

V

Day one

Corumbá de Goiás, October 15, 2018.

***"O que vale na vida não é o ponto de partida e sim a caminhada. Caminhando e semeando, no fim, terás o que colher."* Cora Coralina**

"What is worth in life is not the starting point, but the walk. Walking and sowing, in the end, you will have what to reap." Cora Coralina

Monday. The week began cloudy and lazy for the residents of Corumbá de Goiás. I was feeling stressed out, more than the day before. I woke up in fast pace. Adrenaline got me out of bed early. In a few minutes I would be pedaling alone, willing and prepared to face anything that would come ahead.

I closed my panniers and left the inn. I went to a bakery on the BR-414, near the hotel, to have breakfast. I leaned my bike against a wooden column in the balcony, went in and ordered my breakfast: sandwich with egg, ham and cheese, coffee with milk and orange juice.

At 7:30, fed, I climbed the sloping streets of the city to the Nossa Senhora da Penha de França Church.

Nossa Senhora da Penha de França Church

Painted white and blue; wooden doors and windows; two towers; clock embedded in the window of the tallest tower; two palm trees in front. This beautiful church is an example of the construction system used in the early years of occupation of the Brazilian Midwest. It has wide walls of pylon mud, stone and adobe, large doors and windows, altar full of details. Its construction began in 1750. In 1755 it received a life-size baroque image of its patron saint, who was brought from Portugal. In the following year, during procession, the image fell from the stand and broke. The image that is on the church's altar today is not so big. It was given by a city resident after the accident.

\- - -

I stopped in front of the church, leaned the bike against the staircase wall and prayed for protection for what was to come. What did the Way of Cora Coralina have reserved for me? Just over 350 kilometers of adventure separated me from the City of Goiás.

I left the church's square following Comendador Félix Curado Street, with its beautiful colonial houses. The architectural ensemble of Corumbá was declared a Brazilian Cultural Heritage in 2004. I went down Francisco Miranda Street and went right into Eurico Curado Street. At the end of this street is the portal of the Way of Cora Coralina and the first plaque with excerpts of her texts and poetry that accompany the traveler throughout the journey. Cora would keep me company through her verses.

> *"O que vale na vida não é o ponto de partida e sim a caminhada. Caminhando e semeando, no fim, terás o que colher."* Cora Coralina.

> *"What is worth in life is not the starting point, but the walk. Walking and sowing, in the end, you will have what to reap."* Cora Coralina.

Wise Cora! If I wanted to get there fast, I would drive a car. I like the way, not the arrival!

I passed a wooden bridge, new and well-made, for pedestrians, over the Bagagem Stream, and on the other side, in a small wood, I followed by the Cava, old path, used by the miners and first city inhabitants. It is an eroded passage, the original ground level is two meters above the trail floor, hence the name "Cava", which means ditch, pit.

I left Cava in a part of the city on the banks of the GO-225 Highway. I crossed it and, on the other side, I followed by São João Village. It's a hard ascent by the streets, less than one kilometer. At the end of the village, the slope relieves, the paved streets end and I left the urban perimeter of Corumbá. The dirt road continues going up for two kilometers, before starting to go down to the Prata Stream. I passed the Prata bridge, in the shadow of the riparian forest. Then, there is an interesting area of *cerrado*, where I found a lot of cashews. A toucans couple welcomed me in this part.

> *"Nasci para escrever, mas, o meio, o tempo, as criaturas e fatores outros, contramarcaram minha vida. Sou mais doceira e cozinheira do que escritora, sendo a culinária a mais nobre de todas as Artes: objetiva, concreta, jamais abstrata, a que está ligada à vida e à saúde humana."* Cora Coralina

> *"I was born to write, but the environment, the time, the creatures and other factors, contradicted my life. I am more of a confectioner and a cooker than a writer, and cooking is the noblest of all arts: objective, concrete, never abstract, the one that is linked to the life and human health."* Cora Coralina

When *cerrado* was over, I crossed a farm. It was my first contact with loose cattle in this trip. You have to take it easy because you will never know the reactions that animals will have. The cows left the path when they saw me coming.

> *"E um dia bem distante a mim tu voltarás. E no canteiro materno de meu seio tranquilo dormirás. Plantemos a roça. Lavremos a gleba. Cuidemos do ninho, do gado e da tulha. Fartura teremos e donos de sítio felizes seremos."* Cora Coralina

> *"And one day far away to me you will return. And in the mother's bed of my quiet womb you will sleep. Let's plant the swidden. Let's plough the glebe. Let's take care of the nest, the cattle and the granary. Plenty we will have and happy farm owners we will be."* Cora Coralina

Leaving this farm, I reached the BR-414 Highway, the same that crosses Corumbá de Goiás. I took the highway towards the Corumbá Falls.

> *"Sobrevivi, me recompondo aos bocados, à dura compreensão dos rígidos preconceitos do passado."* Cora Coralina

> *"I survived, recomposing myself to pieces, to the harsh understanding of the rigid prejudices of the past."* Cora Coralina

It was four kilometers up the highway to the viewpoint of Corumbá Falls. There is a bar on the side of the road, on a wooden platform. Privileged place to contemplate the great Corumbá Falls.

Corumbá Falls (Salto Corumbá)

There is no way to pass the BR-414, towards Brasília, and not be amazed by the landscape that appears on the right side of the highway, a few kilometers after the city of Corumbá. The river, which rises at the foot of the Pireneus Hills, forms its first major jump when it reaches the trough formed between hills Bocaina and Olho d'Água. The place is called Corumbá Falls (Salto Corumbá) because the river makes a big leap, but there are several waterfalls in this site and each has its own name.

The first one, with fifty meters of waterfall, is the Salto Waterfall. At its base there was a great pool, deep, full of gravel and gold. It gained the name of Rich Well (Poço Rico) and awakened the greed of the miners of the 19th century. They did not hesitate: using dynamite they opened a rift in the rock, diverting the course of the river to extract from there the precious metal. Thus, the Waterfall of the Golden Throat of The Rich Well was born (Cachoeira da Garganta do Ouro do Poço Rico), a pompous name used to disguise the environmental tragedy consummated there.

There are also other waterfalls, such as Gold Waterfall (Cachoeira do Ouro) and Grotto Waterfall (Cachoeira da Gruta), a camping site and an inn.

- - -

It was 8:30 in the morning. I drank coconut water and rested.

> *"A escola passa o saber e a vida nos dá a sabedoria."* Cora Coralina

> *"School passes on knowledge and life gives us wisdom."* Cora Coralina

Returning to pedal, I climbed the highway for three kilometers, until crossing it and returning to dirt roads. I passed some farms and crossed the Capitão do Mato Stream (Slave Catcher Stream). After the stream, in front of a rehabilitation center for drug users, I passed through a wire gate and followed the path that goes towards the Pirineus Park (Parque dos Pirineus).

There are no defined landmarks on the park boundaries, but the vegetation change is noticeable. Native fields and *cerrado* come to dominate the landscape.

Pirineus State Park (Parque Estadual dos Pirineus)

The Pirineus Park is a conservation unit of the State of Goiás. It covers areas of Pirenópolis, Cocalzinho de Goiás and Corumbá de Goiás, and preserves inside its boundaries one of Brazilian's major drainage divider. To the north, the waters flow through Tocantins/Araguaia drainage basin, and to the South, through Paraná/Prata drainage basin. The waters that flow from the park supply important rivers of the region, such as Corumbá and “das Almas”, which cuts through the city of Pirenópolis. It also houses the Pirineus Peaks, a set of hills that gave name to the park and to the city of Pirenópolis, and Cabeludo Hill, an interesting rocky hill that seems to be composed of a huddle of quartzite columns.

Pirineus or Pireneus?

Spanish immigrants who arrived in the region found similarity between this Goian peaks and the mountain range that divides France and Spain and decided to give it the same name: Pyrenees (Pirineus). In Portuguese, the two spellings are correct, and the writing with an "e" is more common. I preferred to use the name with an "i" because it’s what appears in the state law that created the park.

- - -

I was on top of the plateau. From there, you can see Cocalzinho de Goiás to the northwest, below, on the banks of the Corumbá River. I kept going up. As you enter the park, the vegetation gets denser.

The park is very interesting. Go through it with no hurry. Pay attention to the details of the *cerrado* vegetation and forests, see, listen and feel the springs, drink water in the fountains, contemplate the shape of the rocks in the rock fields, see the types of soil on which you are stepping.

On the path sides there was cashew trees (cajuí). I rode slowly, collecting and eating. I took a lonely path. The peak got bigger and bigger. I arrived at the headquarters area of the park. I encountered a cyclist couple on the main park road, they were coming from Cocalzinho. As I passed through the front of the headquarters, where there are always security guards, a motorcyclist passed by me. I greeted him, as well as the security guard who was on duty. The biker stopped at the head house and started talking with the security guard. I kept going up.

After the head house, the path continues to go up between the hills until it reaches a wide area between them. There are trails to climb the peaks. I searched a well-hidden place in the woods and locked my bike with a padlock, fastening it in a tree. I was right in front of Pirineus Peak.

> *"Saiu o Semeador a semear. Semeou o dia todo e a noite o apanhou ainda com as mãos cheias de sementes. Ele semeava tranquilo, sem pensar na colheita, porque muito tinha colhido do que outros semearam. Jovem, seja você esse semeador. Semeia com otimismo. Semeia com idealismo as sementes vivas da Paz e da Justiça."* Cora Coralina

> *"The Sower came out to sow. He sowed all day and the night caught him still with his hands full of seeds. He soed quietly, without thinking of the harvest, because much had harvested from what others sowed. Young man, be that sower. Sow with optimism. Sow with idealism the living seeds of Peace and Justice."* Cora Coralina

I got on the trail that leads to the top taking only the cameras. The trail is short and easy, despite climbing the hill that was once considered the highest Brazilian peak. It goes around it until it reaches the top, where there is a small chapel dedicated to the Holy Trinity. From above, on clear nights, it is possible to see the lights of several cities in the region, including those of Brasilia. The surrounding hills, paths crossing the savannah and some singletracks streaking the park's vegetation in white make up an unforgettable view.

Pirineus Peak (Pico dos Pirineus)

Pirineus Peak is the second highest point in the State of Goiás. In 1892, the Cruls Commission, which toured the region to demarcate the square where the Federal District would be built, was at the peak to determine its altitude. At that time, some scientists claimed that the peak was the highest point in Brazil, with three thousand meters of altitude. The measurement was made and the question resolved. Actual altitude: 1,385 meters.

\- - -

I stayed a few minutes at the top. Worried about my hidden things, I kept an eye on the movement at the bottom. The position at the top is privileged. At the end of the open area between the hills was a van parked under the trees.

The motorcyclist I had met on arrival passed by, went to the car, circled it and came back. He stopped the motorcycle and started climbing the peak. Seeing him going up, I decided to go down. I found the biker halfway down, on the hill part facing Cocalzinho. I talked to him, who reported seeing a couple inside the van. It was hot in there! He also said that full moon nights are very busy at the Pireneus Peak. I finished the descent, rescued my bike from the middle of the bush and made my way.

I went back the same way for two kilometers, passing through the head house and crossing the main road of the park. Soon after, I entered a singletrack on the right.

> *"Numa ânsia de vida eu abria o vôo nas asas impossíveis do sonho."* Cora Coralina

> *"In a longing for life I opened the flight in the impossible wings of the dream."* Cora Coralina

The beginning of this singletrack, which cuts the south of the park, is a bit difficult for cyclists. There is a lot of rocks, some steps. I passed pushing my bicycle. The difficult section is just over five hundred meters long. Soon, the trail becomes flat and it is possible to pedal easily. Cabeludo Hill (Hairy Hill) started to keep me company on my left side. I passed by a beautiful spring, forming a small waterfall of crystal-clear waters that feed a *buritizal* with half a dozen palm trees. It is one of the springs of the Serra Stream (Hills Stream), which feeds Capitão do Mato Stream.

Coming out of the stream, I climbed a little, and when the landscape opened, I saw another stream. This time, they were the springs of the Capitão do Mato Stream, a tributary of the Corumbá River that belongs to the Platinum Drainage Basin. It is the place known as Sonrisal, which has several falls and small pools of clear and icy waters.

"Ajuntei todas as pedras que vieram sobre mim. Levantei uma escada muito alta e no alto subi. Teci um tapete floreado e no sonho me perdi. Uma estrada, um leito, uma casa, um companheiro. Tudo de pedra. Entre pedras cresceu a minha poesia. Minha vida... Quebrando pedras e plantando flores." Cora Coralina

"I gathered all the stones that came upon me. I lifted a very high ladder and I climbed it on top. I weaved a flowery carpet and in the dream I got lost. A road, a bed, a house, a companion. All made of stone. Among stones grew my poetry. My life ... Breaking stones and planting flowers." Cora Coralina

At this trail point, there is an important detail of the Brazilian geography. Less than five hundred meters separate the spring of Capitão do Mato Stream and one of the springs of "das Almas" River. This short distance makes a huge difference to the path that the waters will follow. This happens because the "das Almas" River belongs to the Tocantins-Araguaia Basin, which ends its journey in the Marajó Bay, in northern Brazil. The Capitão do Mato, which is part of the Platina Basin, will finish its journey in the Prata River, in the South, on the border between Uruguay and Argentina. Waters that spring so close, but follow opposite paths.

When I arrived at the Sonrisal, a young couple came walking along with me. They came by car to the park to see the place. Then, two cyclists passed by taking the opposite way to mine. They asked about the status of the markings (Cora's footprints), that until then were perfect. I took the opportunity to drink some water from the stream and also filled my bottle in case of emergency. The day was very hot and I had already consumed half the water of my camelbak. After meeting the Sonrisal, its pools, falls and stone bridges, I climbed the trail and crossed the major drainage divider, leaving the Platina Basin and entering the Tocantins-Araguaia Basin.

The path gets more closed from there. Preserved riparian forests provide good shade. Sometimes, the path is by singletracks in the middle of the forest, following streams, others are by little used paths. Thus, I crossed small tributaries of the “das Almas” River by ford and the Barriguda Stream by bridge. It is a very beautiful and isolated area.

After crossing the Barriguda, I reached the access road to the Abade Waterfall. That was when I got lost for the first time, despite having the tracklog and being attentive to the markings. The footprints were gone, and when I looked at the GPS, I was off course. The place where the tracklog followed had no sign of trail, only closed bush. I went back and forth several times. I was about to give up and head straight to Pirenópolis, but I decided to go back to find the footprints again, to try to get back on track. I came back until I found a footprint, where I stopped and returned. I followed very carefully, but, likewise, at the junction with the Abade's road, the footprints were gone.

Still in the middle of the junction, I was determined to open the *cerrado* with my hands to follow the path indicated by my GPS, however, fortunately, when I looked at a fence that went up the hill, I saw something yellow painted on a fence post. There was the missing signal. The trail was off the tracklog about thirty meters.

I climbed the trail along the fence to the top of the hill, pushing the bike because there are very steep parts. At the top there was another fence. Fortunately, the bottom wire of this fence was broken and I managed to get the bike under.

I started to go down the Pirineus Hills softly. The trail follows the ridge of the hill that at the top has *cerrado*. It's a wonderful section! Enjoy the sights.

As I went down, I entered into wet areas of forest, full of springs that feed the Barriguda. One of these areas has its name written on a plaque: Daiana's Valley. I went down the Barriguda valley until I reached the quarries area of Pirenópolis. This section, between Abade and the quarries, is even more isolated than the previous one, with eroded paths. I found no living soul. In fact, I did: I surprised two dogs that slept next to the trail. They ran out barking. I do not know who got scared the most, them or me.

I crossed the Barriguda for the last time in the drinking water source that supplies Pirenópolis. It is a beautiful place. Crystal-clear waters flow between the stones. The crystal-brown water, traversed by the sun, makes the white rocks of the river bottom become golden. I took the opportunity to refill my camelbak and renew the bottle water. Unintentionally, I transpose waters from the Platina Basin to the Tocantins-Araguaia Basin. Do you remember I had filled my bottle in the Capitão do Mato Stream? So, I dumped it into the Barriguda.

How good it is to drink water when you're very thirsty. I drank the river water and spent a few minutes resting under the shade of trees.

The path continues going down. Pirenópolis appears in the landscape for the first time, between the hills, at the bottom of the valley.

A plaque indicated that I was entering the Avalon Refuge. The path descends to "das Almas" River. Again, I went through the ford. In this place there is no road, the riverbed is rocky. On the other side, there is a hill to be climbed. It seems impossible, but there is a trail. It is amazing the difference between the relief of the two river sides. I made a big effort to get the bike up the hill.

Cora Coralina's poetry, fixed at the highest point of the trail, revives the weary visitor:

> *"Luta, a palavra vibrante que levanta os fracos e determina os fortes. Quem sentirá a Vida destas páginas ... Gerações que hão de vir de gerações que vão nascer."* Cora Coralina

> *"Fight, the vibrant word that lifts the weaks and determines the strongs. Who will feel the Life of these pages ... Generations to come from generations that will born."* Cora Coralina

I passed the Avalon Refuge and, following the path shaded by the forest, I reached the Pirineus Park Highway.

I crossed the highway and followed the dirt road on the other side, the Waterfalls Road. It crosses the "das Almas" River and gives access to some waterfalls and to the municipal quarry. At 1:30 p.m., I arrived at the Sombra da Mata Campsite cabin. I asked if the restaurant would be open, and fortunately it was. I went to it and had lunch there. I ordered a set meal that was great. I spent almost an hour resting.

I left the campsite going up the road, to the municipal quarry. That is where the Gold Trail begins.

I went into the quarry area, ceded to Coopedras, a cooperative that brings together small miners from the city. The damage is great in the area. There are gigantic mounds of stone and sand. It's from these quarries that come out tons of quartzite, name of the rock popularly known as Pirenópolis Stone or Goian Stone. The municipal quarry is the largest and oldest in the city. Mining began in the colonial period, when quartzite was used by *bandeirantes* as building material, serving as foundation, wall and even roof for houses. Currently, quartzite is mainly used as flooring and decorative coating.

Gold Trail (Trilha do Ouro)

The Gold Trail was the route used by prospectors and workers in the 18th and 19th centuries to reach the mines in Pirineus Hills. Between the quarry and the city, the Gold Trail is a singletrack that follows the banks of "das Almas" River, in the shadow of the riparian forest, passing through several interesting points, with beautiful views of the river and sections of dense forest. Lajeado Well is the best place to swim.

- - -

I followed the road that bordered the quarry until, after a bend, I reached a suspension bridge over the "das Almas" River. Thunders echoing through the valley announced that rain was coming. The bridge was a little crooked. I passed cautiously, but with no fright. It swings, of course. Across the river, I faced unexpected challenges. I had to jump about ten fences. There are "v" pass-through gates, those that allow humans to pass, but hold back the cattle. The bike with panniers does not pass. It's very hard to jump these fences alone, without help. The saddlebags change the bike's center of gravity, making lifting difficult. It's handlebars turning fast and hitting the head, bike unbalancing, tire on the face. In each fence a new battle.

Very well maintained, the trail has bridges and wooden ramps at the most difficult crossing points, such as ditches and small streams. In one of them, there's only a trunk whose upper part has been flattened, but does not fit two feet side by side. It is a balancing exercise. I held the bike with only one hand and passed with maximum attention. It is only three meters long, but they are unforgettable.

Despite being Monday, on almost the entire length of the Gold Trail, people refreshed themselves in the river. I was meeting a lot of people on the banks and in the water, in the various wells, pools and rapids. I also crossed paths with a family of capuchin monkeys who crossed the river jumping over the trees.

Fences, bridges, trunks and ditches overcomed, I arrived in Pirenópolis around 3:30 pm. I went to the Rosário Mother Church where I officially finished the pedal of the day.

I went, then, looking for lodging. After a few laps through downtown, I ended up staying at the Batihá Inn, on the street in front of the "das Almas" River.

It was very hot and I could not resist the call of the river passing there in front of me. I kept the bike in the room and went to take a refreshing bath. Then I returned to the hotel, took a shower and went for a walk through the Pirenópolis' historical town.

Pirenópolis

The city was born in 1727, when Manoel Rodrigues Tomar, head of a group of prospectors submitted to the *bandeirante* Anhanguera and guided by Urbano do Couto Menezes, arrived in the region with the mission of discovering new gold deposits. Initially, it was named Arraial das Minas de Nossa Senhora do Rosário de Meia Ponte (Mines of Our Lady of the Rosary of Half Bridge Hamlet), because a flood brought down half the bridge over the "das Almas" River. The city grew due to mining activity. At that time, most of the population was composed of black people and Brazilian natives, slave labor used in the mines.

With the depletion of the gold deposits, the city's growth stagnated. Only in the 19th century did Pirenópolis grow again, with its economy leveraged by agriculture, livestock and trade.

It gained the name Pirenópolis in 1890 due to the Pirineus Hills.

In the 20th century, tourism boosted again the growth of the city. Keeping its original feature and traditions preserved, Pirenópolis was declared National Historical Heritage in 1988.

It is hard to compete with Pirenópolis in terms of tourism. The city is surrounded by the green of the woods and framed by mountains. Through the *cerrado* and forests of the city flow rivers of crystal-clear waters that form awesome waterfalls. To the east is the Pirineus Hills, guarded by Pirineus Park, with trails, viewpoints and waterfalls. But if all of this is not enough, it still has the historical town, with beautiful churches and colonial houses preserved. The Rua do Lazer (Leisure Street), with dozens of restaurants and bars, buzzes on weekends, and the commerce, which occupies most of the colonial houses in the town, has a lot to show tourists, such as jewelry, handicrafts, decorative objects, clothes, souvenirs. The hotel chain has options to suit every budget, and the proximity of great cities like Brasília and Goiânia facilitates the access of tourists.

- - -

After taking a bowl of açaí-berry and a very iced *cupuaçu* juice, I returned to the inn because the rain threatened to fall hard. I took the opportunity to sleep. When it stopped raining, already at night, I went again to downtown for dinner.

Day summary: 55 kilometers traveled with 1,125 meters of ascent.

VI

Day two

Pirenópolis, October 16, 2018.

***"Sobrevivi, me recompondo aos bocados, à dura compreensão dos rígidos preconceitos do passado."* Cora Coralina**

"I survived, recomposing myself to pieces, to the harsh understanding of the rigid prejudices of the past." Cora Coralina

I didn't wait for the hotel's breakfast. As I was the only guest, I negotiated the price and got a discount, making it better for everyone. At 6:30 a.m., I left. I stopped at the Rosary Church to register the leave. The sky was cloudy, as the day before, but it didn't look like it would rain.

Rosary Mother Church (Igreja Matriz do Rosário)

The construction began in 1728, which characterizes it as the oldest church in the State of Goiás. In 1941, it was declared a National Historical and Artistic Heritage. In 2002, it was destroyed by a fire, going through a thorough restoration process which was done in 2006. Internally, it has works of art such as the paintings of the tabled ceiling, carved wooden statues laminated in gold, altar full of details.

I am always impressed by the width of the walls of these old churches. Those in Our Lady of Rosary Church, the Pirenópolis' Mother Church, are the widest I have ever seen: 1.80 meter thick and 10 meters high. They are made of pylon mud, technique that uses mortar made of earth, gravel, cattle manure and vegetal fibers, mixed and punched with pestle in board molds.

The roof is covered by tiles-thighs. In the Brazilian colonial period, sick or disabled slaves to do heavy works were employed in lighter tasks. Common activity was to produce clay tiles by molding them into their thighs. As each slave had thighs of different sizes and shapes, the tiles were uneven and the roof was crooked after being assembled, apparently badly done. Hence the Brazilian expression “made in the thighs”, that we use to this day to characterize improvised things, ill-done. It is unlikely that the mother church tiles were made on the slaves' thighs as some are more than one meter long. They must have used wooden or clay molds.

- - -

I went to the nearest bakery for breakfast. I ordered the same menu as the day before and also a sandwich for lunch. After eating, as I prepared to leave, a city boy approached and began talking to me, asking where I was going. He was supposed to be at school if he studied in the morning, and that was what I asked him. He said he had to miss to exchange a defective flash drive he bought at a city store. Priorities! When I started to advise him on his studies, he made up some excuse and said goodbye. Kids are funny. I felt old.

I left. Despite knowing Pirenópolis for so many years, I had never passed through the streets where the tracklog took me, tortuous streets in peripheric neighborhoods. I left the city by the southwest, by road GO-431. It was seven kilometers of paved road.

> *"Eu sou aquela mulher a quem o tempo muito ensinou. Ensinou a amar a vida. Não desistir da luta. Recomeçar na derrota. Renunciar a palavras e pensamentos negativos. Acreditar nos valores humanos. Ser otimista."* Cora Coralina

> *"I'm that woman to whom time taught a lot. Taught to love life. Not to give up the fight. To*

> *start over in defeat. To renounce negative words and thoughts. To believe in human values. To be optimistic."* Cora Coralina

I went on the dirt road going down to the Godinho Stream. Despite the previous day rain, the sandy ground path was firm, mudless. Soon, it began to appear sections of forest. Some I just bordered, others I crossed. They are preserved remnants of Goian "Mato Grosso" (thick bush), central state area whose vegetation has dense forests with large trees, such as *mogno*, *jequitibá* and *peroba*, contrasting with the rest of Goiás, where *cerrado* phytophysiognomies predominate. This fantastic forest was devastated from the 1940s, when the Brazilian President Getúlio Vargas created the campaign "Marcha para o Oeste" (march to the west), to occupy scant populated areas of the Brazilian Midwest, where there were many no-owner lands.

A section of forest in a foothill of Godinho Hills was the first challenge of the day. I went up in no hurry. It seemed to be a much insulated place, but a motorcyclist passed by me, breaking the solitude. Coming down, I crossed the Godinho Stream by bridge. Right after the stream, I passed through closed gate and pasture area. The cattle kept a close eye, but I did not have to go through the animals. The trail turned right and went on the other way.

I followed the path in the middle of the pasture and soon reached a corral. The corral, right in front a farm house, was full of cows. The trail passed exactly through its gate. There was nobody close to me to ask if I could pass. I approached the gate, tried to disperse the cows away, but they did not move their feet. By the look of things and by the bellow, they were waiting for the morning feed. What if I opened the gate and the cows ran away? I could even try to pass the corral by the left side, but I would have to jump two barbed wire fences and would have to remove the panniers for that. I decided to face the cows. There were ten, some lying down, some standing. They all looked at me and ruminated with disdain. Tension in the air! I carefully opened the door, tied with a rope, pulled the bike in, leaned it against the fence. No cow got away. I closed the gate, took the bike and pushed it between the cows. It was like I was not there. They did not move a paw from the place and stared at me with their cow faces.

Then, I went through pastures and forests until I reached the Pedras River (Stones River), where the trail enters through the dense riparian forest. The path narrows, goes swerving from the trees until the river bank. When I arrived, I immediately concluded that I would have problems. On this site there is a small half-moon shaped dam, used to move waterwheel. On the opposite bank, the wheel was immobile, but it still made it difficult to pass through the side wall. The best option would be to pass over the dam, however, it was not wide enough to pass pushing the bike. Unbalancing over it would mean falling upstream, into the water, watching the bike go to the bottom; or, fall downstream, hurting myself on the rocks. There was no way: I had to remove the panniers. It was easier with a weightless bike. I passed with the bicycle resting on my shoulder, sliding through the available space over the side wall not occupied by the waterwheel and left the bike in a safe place. I went back and crossed with the panniers.

There are quotes about the Pedras River dating from the 18th century, characterizing it as an excellent resting place, with abundant water and good pastures for animals.

Across the river, the trail continued bordering a fence inside the woods. Before replacing the panniers, I climbed a few meters to see if there would be another fence that I would have to jump, but I didn't see any. I put the panniers back and climbed pedaling. However, two hundred meters later, arriving at a road that crossed the forest, there was a fence, brand new and well-made, with no possibility of going underneath. I landed the cargo again, passed it over, then the bike and jumped the fence.

I followed the road crossing the woods. The hills around gave signs that there would be good climbs ahead. And it didn't take long to get to a steep hill, the worst of the day: Caxambu Hills. Since the passage through the Pedras River, the trail had been going up, but the hill really began when I reached kilometer 22. The trail enters through the hills' forest. Dirt ground at the beginning, which becomes gravel as it rises. The path is pretty, but it was very hot. Protected by *cerradão*, no breeze enters. The average slope of the steepest part is 10%.

At the top, after leaving the *cerradão*, the trail followed *by singletracks* through another pasture area. A few miles later, when I returned to the woods, there was a viewpoint, from where I contemplated the landscape I would ride next.

> *"Creio numa força imanente que vai ligando a família humana numa corrente luminosa de fraternidade universal. Creio na solidariedade humana. Creio na superação dos erros e angústias do presente."* Cora Coralina

> *"I believe in an immanent force that connects the human family in a luminous chain of universal brotherhood. I believe in human solidarity. I believe in overcoming the errors and anguish of the present."* Cora Coralina

The descent of the Caxambu Hills is worse than the ascent: -15% of average slope. If your bike is loaded, you have to go down pushing. The trail zigzags through the slope, passing through ditches and steps, until reaching the base. The descent of the hill continues even after leaving the woods. There's another fence to jump over when the path flattens. This time, I managed to pass the bike over without removing the panniers because the smooth wire fence was low. I passed through the entrance of a farm house and continued down to Caxambu River.

> *"Lua que manda na semeadura dos campos, na germinação das sementes, na abundância das colheitas. Lua boa. Lua ruim. Lua de chuva. Lua de sol."* Cora Coralina

> *"Moon that rules the sowing of fields, the germination of seeds, the abundance of crops. Good moon. Bad moon. Rain moon. Sun moon."* Cora Coralina

At thirty kilometers of pedal, I arrived in the Caxambu Village, belonging to the municipality of Pirenópolis. Caxambu was born in 1948. It has paved streets, bars and grocery stores. Annually, a party is held in honor of the Divine Eternal Father, with a parade of ox carts.

I stopped at the first grocery store I found, which seemed to be the largest of the place. I bought potato chips and soda and sat on a cement bench in front of the store, on the sidewalk. When I started eating, a short, skinny, barefoot, dirty man, who had been there since I arrived, approached and stared at the potatoes packet. He did not say anything. Total concentration in the potatoes. I asked him if he would like some and he promptly accepted making a positive sign with his head. I asked him a few questions, he grumbled and gestured. Apparently, he is one of those mad-people, so common in small towns. With so much appetite, I immediately gave him all the packet. He ate more than half my chips packet and left without thanking me when it ended.

Five kilometers from Caxambu is Babylon Farm (Fazenda Babilônia).

Babylon Farm (Fazenda Babilônia)

Declared a National Historical Heritage, the farm was born as Engenho São Joaquim (Saint Joaquim Mill) in the 18th century. It was founded by the young Joaquim Alves de Oliveira, born in Pilar de Goiás, who studied in São Paulo.

At the age of 25, Joaquim arrived in the then Meia Ponte (Pirenópolis) bringing the fortune that he made trading in Rio de Janeiro. Although the village was in decline due to the depletion of gold mines, by Meia Ponte passed important roads coming from the main cities of that time. Joaquim saw there a great opportunity and started his venture.

The farm planted sugarcane, cassava and cotton on industrial scale. Cotton, exported to England, was considered the best in the world. The farm came to have two hundred slaves and was the largest agricultural company in Goiás at that time. The income generated by the enterprise was often higher than the income of the then province.

To make the production flow, the *Comendador* (Commander), as he came to be known, created great troop of mules. With this troop, he transported not only his production, but also the ones of other farms and cities to the consumers markets. In return, the animals brought scarce products inland, generating huge profits from the trade.

The farm eventually decayed after the death of the Comendador's wife and some children. He passed away at the age of 81. It was Priest Simeão who acquired the lands of Joaquim's heirs and gave the farm the name Babylon. When visiting the farm and seeing the large number of aggregates and slaves, the priest thought it resembled the historical Babylon.

Today the farm is dedicated to livestock and tourism.

- - -

The Cora Way does not pass through Babylon Farm, requiring detour and time to visit it. I didn't come through there.

I paid my bill at the grocery store and went back to action. I crossed Caxambu and followed the path, passing through several streams and the Padre Souza River.

"O saber se aprende com mestres e livros. A sabedoria, com o corriqueiro, com a vida e com os humildes." Cora Coralina

"Knowledge is acquired from masters and books. Wisdom, with the commoner, with life and with the humble." Cora Coralina

I arrived at the Transbrasiliana Highway nine kilometers after Caxambu. I followed the highway for just over a kilometer and went back to dirt roads.

"Eu sou a ramada dessas árvores, sem nome e sem valia, sem flores e sem frutos, de que gostam a gente cansada e os pássaros vadios." Cora Coralina

"I am the branch of these trees, without name and without value, without flowers and without fruits, that like tired people and stray birds." Cora Coralina

I crossed the Degredo and Santo Antônio streams to reach Radiolândia, another village belonging to Pirenópolis, with 48 kilometers pedaled on the day.

"Já bebi água do rio na concha da minha mão. Fui velha quando era moça. Tenho a idade de meus versos. Acho que assim fica bem. Sou velha namoradeira. Lancei a rede na lua, ando catando as estrelas." Cora Coralina

> *"I already drank river water in the shell of my hand. I was old when I was a girl. I am as old as my verses. I guess that's fine. I am an old flirtatious. I threw the cast net on the moon, I have been picking up the stars."* Cora Coralina

The small Radiolândia was born in 1952, when an allotment was made and a church was built. At first, it was called Rabeia Bode, a name that has no clear explanation. Fact is that no one liked the old name and is considered offencive by some older residents. In the 1960s, Transbrasiliana crossed the village, being later transferred.

> *"Dai, Senhor, que minha humildade seja como a chuva desejada caindo mansa, longa noite escura, numa terra sedenta e num telhado velho. Que eu possa agradecer a Vós, minha cama estreita, minhas coisinhas pobres, minha casa de chão, pedras e tábuas remontadas. E ter sempre um feixe de lenha debaixo do meu fogão de taipa, e acender, eu mesma, o fogo alegre da minha casa na manhã de um novo dia que começa."* Cora Coralina

> *"Give, Lord, may my humility be like the desired rain falling gently, long dark night, in a thirsty land and on an old roof. May I thank You, my narrow bed, my poor little things, my earthen floor house, stones and reassembled boards.* And always have a bundle of firewood under

> my rammed earth stove, *and light up, myself, the joyful fire of my house on the morning of a new day that begins."* Cora Coralina

I stopped at Miranda Market, in front of the Chapel of Saint Michael the Archangel. It was 12:30 p.m. I decided to have lunch there. The market is small. Tiago is the name of the current owner. The family business started with your grandparents. I bought a soda and sat on the bench built next to the front wall of the building. It was very hot, so I took off my shirt, helmet, gloves and shoes. I was not too hungry, but I still took the sandwich and opened a can of tuna. When Tiago saw me eating, he offered lunch. His grandmother had prepared and as only the two of them had lunch, there was some left over. I refused to be polite, but I should have accepted. If I had not started eating yet, I'd take it for sure.

Another resident of the city came to the market. He was a man with more than seventy years old who appeared to be slightly drunk. He tried to explain to me why the place was known as Rabeia Bode. I didn't understand the explanation because his diction, influenced by alcohol, was compromised. I only understood that the name motivated many strife when pronounced in the bars of the city.

Thunders began to echo around Radiolândia. Around 1 p.m., I paid my bill and went on my way.

"Sendo eu mais doméstica do que intelectual, não escrevo jamais de forma consciente e raciocinada, e sim impelida por um impulso incontrolável. Sendo assim, tenho a consciência de ser autêntica." Cora Coralina

"Being more housekeeper than intellectual, I never write consciously and reasoned, but driven by an uncontrollable impulse. So, I am consciously authentic." Cora Coralina

The paved road that began when I got into the village ended soon and the dirt road was back. The Paio Velho Stream and "dos Índios" Stream (Indians' Stream) are crossed after the end of the paved road. When leaving a section of forest, after the "dos Índios" Stream, I saw where the thunders were coming from. To my right, there were two mountain ranges: "do Loredo" and "do Chibio". Heavy rains fell on them and the wind brought the first drops to the road where I was. I accelerated to try to escape the water and managed to stay dry for a long stretch. I passed by the Retiro River and the Cocal Stream.

"Sobrevivi, me recompondo aos bocados, à dura compreensão dos rígidos preconceitos do passado." Cora Coralina

"I survived, recomposing myself to pieces, to the harsh understanding of the rigid prejudices of the past." Cora Coralina

Apparently, the route of the old Transbrasiliana was by the road on which I followed, but when it reaches the bank of the Grande Stream (Big Stream), the Cora Way abandons it.

I went by left. I crossed many farms and pastures. In some, passing through the herds was inevitable. I passed carefully, making enough noise for the animals to see me from afar, without surprising them or scaring them. Three kilometers before the Rocinha Stream, the rain reached me. It was thickening until it collapses strong. I stopped under a tree at the top of the slope. As I took shelter, I could see that it was not just me who was bothered by the rain. The farm animals in front of me fled in groups. It was an unusual scene. Cows, sheep, goats and horses ran together, in line, fast-paced downhill, heading to the corral.

I stood there for a few minutes. Thunders roared and I was afraid that some lightning would fall on the tree where I took shelter. I continued the path in the rain, crossed the Rocinha and then the Corumbá Stream. It didn't take long for San Francisco de Goiás to emerge on the horizon. Just before 4 p.m., I crossed the GO-080 Highway and got into San Francisco.

São Francisco de Goiás

São Francisco de Goiás was born in 1740. Prospectors who mined gold in the Jaraguá Hills found fertile land south of the mountains. Several farms were formed and a cluster of houses appeared around a straw chapel where the farmers prayed rosaries in praise of San Francisco. Thus was born the village of São Francisco das Chagas that over the years was changing its name: Arraial das Chagas (Chagas Hamlet), then only Chagas. In 1953, the village was dismembered from Jaraguá and became a municipality with the current denomination.

- - -

There are two hotels on the side of the highway. I chose the Maria Rita Hotel, which is in front of the city hall. I was the only guest. I took the opportunity to wash my bike that was full of mud. I had to share the room with dozens of brown beetles that were scattered all over the city. I tried to kick them out, but the work was innocuous. I trapped most of the beetles inside the bathroom.

After the bath, I went to the market to buy supplies. I had a headache. The three days of long pedals, without feeding me properly, charged their price. I began to consider the possibility of overnighting in Jaraguá.

After it got dark, I had skewers in a diner in front of city hall.

Day summary: 77 kilometers traveled with 1,660 meters of climb.

VII

Day three

São Francisco de Goiás, October 17, 2018.

***"A vida tem duas faces: Positiva e negativa. O passado foi duro mas deixou o seu legado. Saber viver é a grande sabedoria."* Cora Coralina**

"Life has two faces: one positive and one negative. The past was hard but left its legacy. Knowing how to live is the greatest wisdom." Cora Coralina

It rained a lot during the night. I couldn't even sleep properly. When I woke up, at 5:45 a.m., it was still raining, very lightly, but it rained. I got up in a low mood, imagining I would catch mud on the path. The weather forecast presented in the morning news was depressing: there would be storms over the whole region.

I left the hotel at 6:30 with the bike ready. It had stoped raining. I went to the bakery that would serve the hotel breakfast, two hundred meters away.

Despite the forecast, the horizon in front of me was beautiful, with sparse clouds in the sky, but I wouldn't go in that direction, my path was exactly the opposite, to the east. I was still in doubt whether I would go to Itaguari or stay overnight in Jaraguá.

I finished breakfast and when I rode the bike, it started to drizzle again. I started the pedal passing in front of São Francisco's Church. I stopped in front of it and took pictures. When I left, I realized that the front tire was flat. It was the missing sign: I decided to overnight in Jaraguá.

I went back to the gas station, near the hotel where I overnighted, to use the air compressor. It didn't help just filling the tire, I had to change the inner tube.

Task finished, I finally left. Leaving the city, the path has five kilometers of paved road. Long descent that led me to cross the "dos Alves" Brook. Soon after, I entered dirt roads. There was a little mud, but the sandy soil did not let the clay stick to the tires. I passed by the Pari River, then the Gueroba Stream. Most of the route to Jaraguá is through the Pari valley, crossing its tributaries. At 17.5 kilometers I reached the BR-070 Highway, crossed it and continued along the dirt road on the other side.

As I was going to sleep in Jaraguá, I was in no hurry. I'd contemplate the landscape calmly. The day that started gray became clear, the sun came up and illuminated the huge hills on my right, to the east, which I would soon face: the Jaraguá Hills.

I crossed the Caetano's Stream. The road that followed through the middle of farms and pastures showed me examples of the great trees that constituted Mato Grosso Goiano. Isolated groves with trees of long and thick trunks, with high crowns.

> *"Minha identificação profunda e amorosa com a terra e com os que nela trabalham. A gleba me transfigura. Dentro da gleba, ouvindo o mugido da vacada, o mééé dos bezerros. O roncar e focinhar dos porcos, o canto dos galos, o cacarejar das poedeiras, o latir dos cães, eu me identifico. Sou a árvore, sou tronco, sou raiz, sou folha, sou graveto, sou mato, sou paiol e sou a velha tulha de barro."* Cora Coralina

> *"My deep and loving identification with the earth and with those who work on it. The glebe transfigures me. Inside the glebe, listening to the moaning of the cows, the "meh" of the calves. The pigs snoring and nuzzling, the*

roosters crowing, the laying hens cackling, the dogs barking, I identify myself. I'm the tree, I'm trunk, I'm root, I'm leaf, I'm twig, I'm bush, I'm barn and I'm the old clay granary." Cora Coralina

The day was beautiful, despite the forecast of thunderstorms in the afternoon.

As I passed through a section of forest, I found a cowboy driving four cows down the road. I stopped by the side of the path and was quiet waiting for the cows to pass. After the cows passed, the cowboy stopped by my side and thanked me for waiting. According to him, if I had continued, the cows would have fled because they are unsociable. Be very careful with animals!

I went through a pineapple plantation.

"De onde vens, criança? Que mensagem trazes de futuro? Por que tão cedo esse batismo impuro que mudou teu nome?" Cora Coralina

"Where do you come from, child? What message do you have for the future? Why so soon this unclean baptism that changed your name?" Cora Coralina

I crossed the North-South Railway at kilometer 21 of my day. The gauge (distance between the rails) of the railway is wide, different from most of the

Brazilian's railways. The wide gauge allows trains to carry more weight and travel at higher speeds.

Right after the railroad, I crossed the Grande Stream and then the Boa Vista Stream (Good View Stream). I reached another section of the railroad, but this time the passage was by concrete bridge. From above the bridge I had beautiful views of a hill range to the northwest, with three well-highlighted hills whose names I do not know.

I arrived again at the Pari River. I have been following its course from San Francisco and it was time to cross it once again. There was a lot of mud on the concrete bridge. I used the narrow sidewalk on the side, higher and without so much clay, to cross it.

Five hundred meters after, the path makes a sharp turn to the right. There begins the Jaraguá Hills, the most beautiful and difficult path section of the day.

> *"Em mim a planta renasce e floresce, sementeia e sobrevive. Sou a espiga e o grão fecundo que retornam à terra. Minha pena é enxada do plantador, é o arado que vai sulcando para a colheita das gerações. Eu sou o velho paiol e a velha tulha roceira. Eu sou a terra milenária, eu venho de milênios. Eu sou a mulher mais antiga do mundo, plantada e fecundada no ventre escuro da terra."* Cora Coralina

"In me the plant reborns and blooms, sows and survives. I'm the cob and the fruitful grain that returns to earth. My pen is the planter's hoe, it's the plow that furrows for the harvest of generations. I'm the old barn and the old farm granary. I am the millenary land, I come from millennia. I am the oldest woman in the world, planted and fecundated in the dark womb of the earth." Cora Coralina

Jaraguá Hills State Park (Parque Estadual da Serra de Jaraguá)

Jaraguá Hills State Park preserves springs, founts, fauna, flora, scenic beauties and archaeological sites existents in the area of almost three thousand hectares between the municipalities of São Francisco de Goiás and Jaraguá. It's a beautiful place, with preserved forest and stunning views.

\- - -

To better explain how is the climb of Jaraguá Hills, I divided it into five parts.

Jaraguá Hills - Part 1

The first part is 4.5 kilometers long, with an average slope of 5%, maximum of 27%.

The beginning is easy. The road enters through the middle of the *cerrado*, full of fruits at the time of the beginning of the rains. I found a couple there, picking up *pequi* (Brazilian fruit very appreciated by the Goians). At the end of the first climb, I stopped to enjoy the view and rest.

The road continues predominantly rising. Heavy but pedalable sections intersperse with some descents. Everything was going very well. I figured that my friends who passed there before me, who warned me about the difficulty of these hills, just tried to scare me with their reports.

After passing through a stream by the ford, I arrived to a house in front of small dam. It is the temporary place of the park head office, a place known as Maria Helena.

Arrows painted on a tree point to the left. I crossed the small bridge of planks over the dam ebb and, on the other side, behind a bamboo grove, I reached the point where everything changed. That is where things got ugly. The next arrow points up!

Jaraguá Hills - Part 2

Five hundred meters long, with an average slope of 15%, maximum of 38%, immersed in the dense forest of the hill slope.

The narrow trail enters the forest with high slope, bordering the cliff. Falling to the left side could be fatal. If I had the bike without load, it would already be difficult to climb, with load then it seemed impossible. Even wearing MTB shoes, sometimes the support foot escaped, slipping on the gravel, on the dry leaves. I went up meter by meter. Some high steps were the worst parts. It was necessary to lift the bike with all that weight and put it on the upper level, then it was time to lift my body. On one of these steps, a large tree makes more difficult to pass, making the trail even narrower. Meter by meter I won the first phase of the push-bike.

When I left the large forest, the trail became wider and the view opened. I could see a little of the landscape through which I walked: dense forest between the hills.

Jaraguá Hills - Part 3

There are 850 meters of ascent, with an average inclination of 18%, maximum of 33%.

At the top, the large forest gives way to the *cerrado*. The soil, instead of earth and sand, is covered with gravel. I kept pushing the bike hill up. In this part, what stands out is the beauty of the landscape. As you enter the park, the green forest carpet appears to be bigger. There are several steps along the way and most of the trail is on the side of the hills. The effort is great. But in some parts, it is possible to pedal, always very carefully not to tip to the right side, almost a cliff.

Cerrado fruits decorated the trees on the trail side. Lots of *mangaba*, all still green. A good and eatable *mangaba* should be on the ground, where the maturation process ends and there is no more milky sap in the fruit, which makes it bitter. Lots of ripe *cajuí* (little cashew), some of them sweet, but mostly sour. *Pequi* everywhere, but unfortunately, we don't eat raw *pequi*.

I climbed unhurriedly, enjoying the scenery, eating cashews and resting in the rare shadows. Suddenly, an encouraging image unveiled among the trees: the towers at the top of the hill.

Jaraguá Hills – Part 4

It is 630 meters long, with an average inclination of 6.7%, maximum of 12%.

The worst is over. The trail flattens and it's possible to pedal. The towers are nearby.

I climbed up pedaling where I could. The singletrack has many large stones that make it difficult to pass.

The singletrack finally ends on a dirt road that passes through the antennas and reaches the viewpoint of Jaraguá Hills. The suffering is over. I spent long minutes resting, enjoying the view, contemplating the incredible scenery that the lookout point provides to the winners of this challenge.

"A vida tem duas faces: Positiva e negativa. O passado foi duro mas deixou o seu legado. Saber viver é a grande sabedoria. Que eu possa dignificar minha condição de mulher, aceitar suas limitações e me fazer pedra de segurança dos valores que vão desmoronando. Nasci em tempos rudes, aceitei contradições, lutas e pedras como lições de vida e delas me sirvo. Aprendi a viver." Cora Coralina

"Life has two faces: one positive and one negative. The past was hard but left its legacy. Knowing how to live is the great wisdom. May I dignify my woman condition, accept its limitations and make me safety stone of the values that are crumbling. I was born in rude times, I accepted contradictions, fights and stones as life lessons and of them I serve myself. I learned to live." Cora Coralina

Jaraguá Hills - Part 5

After the well-deserved rest, I followed my way to Jaraguá. I went down in ecstasy, enjoying every meter, braking, watching the *cerrado* and looking for *mangabas*. I like *mangaba* a lot. And I was gifted with many of them. I stopped at the *mangaba* trees and looked on the floor for the ripe fruits. I had already eaten so much cashew that I didn't even care for the cashew trees. I even found *bacupari* and *mamacadela*, also *cerrado* fruits, still green.

I was so distracted, I didn't even notice a ditch in front of me. My front tire slipped and I fell. It wasn't anything serious because I was slow.

It was 4.3 kilometers of descent from the viewpoint to the Rosary Church.

Our Lady of the Rosary Church (Igreja de Nossa Senhora do Rosário)

It was built in 1776, on a small elevation away from the center of Jaraguá at that time. It was the blacks' church, because slaves were forbidden to attend celebrations in the church that whites attended, so it was called Blacks' Rosary Church.

Its walls are of pylon mud, clay tiles roof. Internally, the nave has exposed roof timber and carved altars. The side altar is more refined than the main. His belfry, with only two small bells, stands outside. It is made with two wooden beams that hold up the bells and a small roof.

\- - -

I pedaled to downtown. I stopped at Banco do Brasil to withdraw money because what I took was over.

I had lunch in a restaurant next to the bank, very simple, good food, fair price. I put the bike inside the building, in front of the cashier. I was very thirst, so I ordered a jar of *cajá* juice, which only reached the table when I was about to finish eating. It was distressing to wait for the juice so thirsty.

Lunched, I paid the bill and went out looking for a place to stay overnight. After a few laps through downtown, I arrived at the Boa Vista Hotel. Due to the size of the hotel and the sophistication of the facade, I imagined that the daily rate would be expensive. I didn't even dare to enter. I was leaving to continue the search when a hotel employee walked down the sidewalk next to me. I asked her if she knew the room rate. She said it was "a hundred and a few bucks", far less than I thought. I stopped the bike in the *porte-cochère* and went to check. It really wasn't expensive for a day I needed rest. I invested, I stayed!

In addition to being downtown, Boa Vista has a swimming pool, sauna, air conditioning, new and clean rooms. Ideal for a day of rest and a good night of sleep.

They let me go up with the bike to the bedroom. The first step was to take a shower. Then I checked the bicycle brake, which was too low, and patched the punctured inner tube.

The afternoon was lazy: I slept, relaxed by the pool, ate *açaí* with *cupuaçu* in Coreto Plaza, a shake that the snack bar menu calls *Coquetel*. Try this mixture, it's delicious!

At night, I went out in search of a good barbecue, which I found not far from the hotel.

Overnight in Jaraguá was a great decision. Friendly town, welcoming people, first rate hotel with swimming pool, sauna and full breakfast. The good thing about traveling alone is that you can change the trip however you want. In fact, I was not so lonely: Cora Coralina accompanied me with her unexpected verses in the curves of the path.

Day summary: 40 kilometers traveled with 883 meters of climb.

VIII

Day four

Jaraguá, October 18, 2018.

***"Eu sou a dureza desses morros, revestidos, enflorados, lascados a machado, lanhados, lacerados. Queimados pelo fogo. Pastados. Calcinados e renascidos."* Cora Coralina**

"I am the hardness of these hills, coated, bloomed, chipped by axes, lame, lacerated. Burned by fire. Grazed. Calcined and reborned." Cora Coralina

I was able to rest very well. Quiet, comfortable and freezing night. Blessed air conditioning! It didn't rain at night, or I didn't hear it, who cares. When I looked out the bedroom window, the sky was clear, foreshadowing a beautiful sunny day.

Jaraguá

Jaraguá is a friendly city, with wide streets with not much traffic. It has few historic buildings. Born in the *bandeirantes* time, that settled on the banks of Jaraguá Stream, between 1726 and 1728, exploring alluvial gold. In 1748, the Arraial do Córrego do Jaraguá (Jaraguá Stream Hamlet) already had streets and chapel. To supply food to the mines population, farms were created on the hamlet surroundings.

The toponym "Jaraguá" derives from the Tupi-Guarani and means "lord of the valley". Near the place where the community was formed there were a Jaraguá Indians tribe, who lent the name to the hills, the stream and to the then hamlet.

The "March to the West" and the construction of the Belém-Brasília Highway boosted the city growth in the 20th century. In the 1980s, Jaraguá saw the clothing industry grow, which together with agriculture is now its economic base.

- - -

I would have another day of tranquility to pedal unhurriedly to Itaguari. I went up to the breakfast area on the roof of the building. When I arrived and looked southwest, I saw that the weather was not so open in that direction. Although concentrated, heavy rain fell on some mountains in the direction of Pirenópolis. But for now, in the hotel the sun was shining.

I had breakfast without haste. I ate and drank everything I was able. Boa Vista's breakfast was great. I went back to the room, gathered my stuff and went down. At 8:30, I was in front of the Our Lady of Penha Church. I asked for protection for my journey.

Two hundred meters ahead, on the same avenue, there is another church that has been transformed into a museum: Our Lady of Conception Church.

Our Lady of Conception Church (Igreja de Nossa Senhora da Conceição)

It was built in 1828 at the initiative of Antônio de Souza Félix, who had the church built in front of his loft. Its walls are of pylon mud with one meter thick, floor made with wooden boards and mezanela (well-burned brick), clay tiles. It has a rectangular floor plan with only one side gallery. Bell tower and cemetery outside. Near the altar there are five graves and, outside, two, but it is believed that there are more bodies buried.

The entire surroundings of the church were modified, leaving it isolated and seemingly displaced. The side gallery, built to be a warehouse and sacristy, today houses the Jaraguá Museum.

- - -

I continued my journey through Alto do Rosário Street, passing through the Rosary Church and going to the exit of the city. I took a dirt road that goes down the Pari River valley, skirting the Jaraguá Hills from the north and west. I went through the same fork the day before, which gives access to the hills, but I didn't enter it, I went ahead pedaling the opposite way. I passed the Pari River and the North-South Railway. The mud that covered the bridge had dried. Nine kilometers after the Rosary Church, after crossing the Boa Vista Stream, I took a road on the right. From then on, new paths.

I followed farm roads and pastures. At the crossing of a stream, I had another confrontation with loose animals. The passage through the stream is by bridge and its heads have been elevated with earth to keep it out of the reach of the floods. There is a gate over the landfill. Several cows grazed near the stream, on the road and on the sides. One of the cows was right in front of the gate. I approached carefully. The cows left the road and moved away, except the cow at the gate, which was trapped at the top. The ruminant would have to leave because the gate opened to the side where it was. I talked to the cow, gesticulated, asked it to leave, but it didn't understand me. Although cornered, it was calm. I layed the bike on the ground, off the road, and walked on the right side, climbing up the embankment until I reached the gate. Before I even tried to open it, the cow, seeing the road cleared, ran away. I was able to pass calmly.

> *"Graças, Senhor, pelo primeiro semeador que lançou a primeira semente na terra e pelo homem que amassou, levedou e cozeu o primeiro pão. Graças, meu Deus, por essa bandeira branca de Paz que traz a certeza do pão."* Cora Coralina

> *"Thank thee, Lord, for the first sower who threw the first seed in the earth and for the man who kneaded, leavened and baked the first bread. Thank thee, my God, for that white flag of Peace that brings the certainty of the bread."* Cora Coralina

Continuing the path, I crossed the Patos River (Ducks River) and climbed the valley up until Aparecida Village. I stopped at a bar to ease my thirst. Customers talked about the cattle price.

Following the path, I crossed the Água Limpa Creek (Clear Water Creek) and, at 29 kilometers, I arrived in Alvelândia, another small village on the bank of the BR-070 Highway. I stopped at a bar and took Gatorade. I left the village crossing the highway.

> *"Eu sou a dureza desses morros, revestidos, enflorados, lascados a machado, lanhados, lacerados. Queimados pelo fogo. Pastados. Calcinados e renascidos."* Cora Coralina

> *"I am the hardness of these hills, coated, bloomed, chipped by axes, lame, lacerated. Burned by fire. Grazed. Calcined and reborned."* Cora Coralina

Just five kilometers later, I arrived in another village, Palestina, smaller than Alvelândia. In this community I didn't stop.

> *"Amo a terra de um velho amor consagrado através de gerações de avós rústicos, encartados nas minas e na terra latifundiária, sesmeiros. A gleba está dentro de mim. Eu sou a terra. Identificada com seus homens rudes e obscuros, enxadeiros, machadeiros e boiadeiros, peões e moradores."* Cora Coralina

> *"I love the earth of an old consecrated love through generations of rustic grandparents, inserted in the mines and landowner earth, allottees. The glebe is inside me. I am the earth. Identified with its rude and obscure men, tillers, axmen and cowboys, peons and residents."* Cora Coralina

Leaving Palestina, I entered a three-kilometer section of dense forest. I climbed the hill bordering the forest and reached the highest point of the day. I started to come down, first passing through pasture where there were various fallen trees, knocked down by the wind, preventing the passage by the singletrack registered in the tracklog. Then, by rural paths, I passed through some livestock farms. I crossed the Bonsucesso Stream, the Brás Stream and the Sucuri River. Leaving the Sucuri valley, I arrived in Itaguari around 12 p.m.

Itaguari

Although the name of the city appears to be indigenous in origin, it isn't. It is an acronym invented when it was decided to change the name of the then Campestre Village. Initially, the name Itariguá was suggested, being "ita" of Itaberaí, "ri" of Sucuri and "guá" of Jaraguá, but then they chose to change the syllables order.

The city was born when the decay of gold mines in the region led the population engaged in such activity to seek other sources of livelihood, settling in the lands near the Sucuri River and Casa das Telhas Stream (Tiles House Stream).

In 1946, the idea of creating an urban agglomeration arose. Farmers donated land and the Catholic Church founded the village. Around 1966, the Church sold the village to farmers who opened streets and sold lots. Itaguari became a municipality only in 1987.

- - -

I cycled downtown and had lunch in a simple restaurant, which served set meals. Good food, fair price.

After lunch, I went looking for my lodging. There was only one hotel in the city, which was located at Auto Posto Itaguari (Itaguari Gas Station), on the edge of GO-154 Highway. When I arrived, the hotel attendant wasn't there, he had gone to lunch. He came back around 2 p.m., when I was able to check-in.

Itaguari is a quiet town. It would've been better to followed the path to São Benedito, and from there take the road to Itaberaí and spend the night there. I spent the rest of the day between downtown walks and naps. At night, I had dinner in downtown, I ate "jantinha com espetinho" (set meal with barbecue). "Jantinha" is the street food revolution. It has carbohydrate, protein and salad, a complete and tasty meal.

Day summary: 50 kilometers traveled with 895 meters of climb.

IX

Day five

Itaguari, October 19, 2018.

> ***"Todos estamos matriculados na escola da vida, onde o mestre é o tempo."* Cora Coralina**

> *"We are all enrolled in the school of life, where the master is time."* Cora Coralina

When I arrived at the hotel in Itaguari, there were beetles everywhere outside. In my room it was no different. There was less than in the halls, but I figured they would soon come in. During the afternoon and evening they were appearing in greater numbers. I started hunting them. I was putting them in a PET bottle. I filled half the half-liter bottle.

During the night, it rained a lot. In the morning, when I woke up, the rain was still falling. I prayed it would stop while I had coffee. The hotel had breakfast.

Seven o'clock in the morning and the rain continued. The weather forecast was rainy all day and the sky confirmed the gloomy forecast: it was all gray, it wintered!

As it would be a long day of pedal and the weather gave no hope of improvement, I decided to leave. I took the bike from the warehouse, fastened the panniers, took one last look at the sky trying to find some hole in the ceiling of clouds. There was none!

I left the gas station trying the freezing rain. I crossed the GO-154 and a few meters after I went into the dirty road. I was very tense, for sure it was the day when I was most nervous. With rain, the chances of breakdown multiply. The road was soaked, but no sticky mud. The Monjolinho Stream was the first watercourse I crossed on the day.

I followed Cora's footsteps. It didn't take long for me to find differences between my tracklog and the path marked by the yellow footprints. I guided myself by the footprints.

Clouds of flying termites covered the fields I crossed. It's in this humid and hot weather that these alate termites usually fly out to form new colonies. Their strategy of flying in the rain is good, since most predators are sheltered. I went through the flying termites cloud. They went in by the clothes, by the helmet, into the pannier. I accidentally ate some, it tastes awful.

The intensity of the rain alternated. In some moments, it'd become a light drizzle and, in others, a thick cold rain that poked the skin like a needle. I followed cautiously, choosing very carefully the space with less mud on the road to pass.

After crossing the Moraes Stream, I bordered the riparian forest of its neighbor Jardim Stream and crossed it by bridge. The exit from this stream was the tensest moment of the day. There was a quagmire on the road, whose mud came out of newly plowed side swiddens. The thick rain formed a heavy flood. After the sloping area and a contour farming, a mud pool was formed. I passed pushing the bike by the fence side, trying to avoid the mud. I managed to cross, but the rest of the road, until I reached the head of the valley, was also with plenty of mud and water. At the top, I passed by a milk transport truck entering the farm. The road was so smooth that it was rolling sideways, it seemed to be drifting, maneuvering to stay in line.

At 25 kilometers I arrived in São Benedito. I entered the village from the south. I passed in front of his modest church.

"Vintém de cobre ... Ainda o vejo, ainda o sinto, ainda o tenho, na mão fechada." Cora Coralina

"Copper vintém ... I still see it, I still feel it, I still have it, in my closed hand."* Cora Coralina

* *vintém* is the name of a antique Portuguese coin

São Benedito (Saint Benedict)

The history of the village is linked to the faith of a man named Benedito, who lived nearby and worked as a craftsman, making clay pans. Devotee of Saint Benedict, he had never seen an image of the saint, until, on a visit to Itaberaí, he gained a Saint Benedict picture. Back at his home, based on the picture, he made a clay statue of Saint Benedict. This image was eventually given to a friend of Benedito, Mrs. Adelaide, who built an altar in her house and began to pray the rosary daily in front of the saint. Over time, some miracles occurred that were attributed to Saint Benedict until, in 1919, the saint won a feast that takes place until today, annually. Residents of nearby towns organized pilgrimages to the then farm. In 1940, the construction of the first chapel began, which encouraged some people to build houses around it, giving rise to the village that was born with the name of Olhos d'Água (Waterholes).

- - -

The GO-156 Highway cuts São Benedito. The surroundings cassava plantations supply the village factories and several shops on the highway display the products in transparent bags. *Tapioca* flour (cassava starch) is what you will see most.

I stopped at a bar that served *tapiocas*. Nothing more convenient for a restaurant in that place. The raw material is abundant.

Up there, I pedaled in the rain. Soaked, I took off my shirt and removed the dozens of flying termites that accompanied me, before they formed colony on my skin. I put on my waterproof coat with nothing underneath, so I wouldn't get cold and my body would dry.

While the *tapioca* didn't arrive, I kept having coffee and talking with the owners. They came from the Brazilian Northeast to work as housekeepers in ranches around the village and ended up settling in the community. As there are no restaurants, they built the bar, which provides meals for lunch and *tapioca* all day. The tapioca was very good, stuffed with ground beef, olives and cheese. It surprised me because the bar was very simple. While I ate, the rain stopped.

I finished eating, paid the bill and left. Just before I left, passed through the front of the bar a fisherman taking his stuff on a cargo bike. I reached him after the limits of the village and we continued pedaling and talking. We passed together by Manoel Brito Stream. He accelerated on the descent of the Noronha Stream. Heavy bikes speed up a lot. Crossing the stream, we took the road on the left and we left the highway. Soon after, we arrived at a balneary on the banks of the Uru River. If I'm not mistaken, the name is Balneário das Pedras (Stones' Balneary). It seems to be a good place to rest, bathe in the river and drink something. The river is full of rocks. My fisherman friend stayed there.

The road followed through the middle of swiddens. I went through several circular crops, irrigated by central pivots. I crossed the São Pedro Creek and soon arrived in Calcilândia, with 47 kilometers of pedal.

Calcilândia

Calcilândia is a one street village on the bank of the GO-522 Highway. Three kilometers from the city, there is a limestone mining company. I am not sure about the origin of the name of the village because I have not found any toponymic study, but I believe it is related to the limestone deposits (*calcário*=limestone).

- - -

Midday. I stopped at a bar at the entrance to the village, in GO-522 side. There were some trucks stopped in front. Due to the mining company, the truck traffic is large. I sat on a bench and took out my lunch: a sandwich I prepared in the morning and a can of tuna. The bar owner was having lunch and even offered me a meal. Once again I missed the opportunity because I wasn't too hungry.

I finished eating and went on my way. The path turns the corner and enters the village, following a dirt road that cuts longitudinally through the long urban area. At the exit of the community there is small stream that passes under the road. In the lower part, it accumulated a lot of clay, the stickiest I found on the journey. I sank into the mud when I went by, got stuck, and had to push the bike out of there. I took as much clay off the wheels as I could and went on my way.

A few hundred more meters and I returned to the highway, in a section without paved road. I followed by it for 1,400 meters until I found a fork. There is sign indicating "Goiás" in front, and also a yellow footprint painted on the fence post. It is not clear which direction to take. I was in doubt and followed the wider road, but I soon realized that I left the tracklog. If I continued, I would pass through the middle of the mining company, which was already close. I went back and took the left narrow road.

There began the best section of the day. The path transposes sections of forest and *cerrado*. I passed the Cabrinha Stream by the ford, where I took the opportunity to remove the clay from the bike, washing its wheels. There began the famous Serra Dourada (Golden Hills). I followed the gap between Cardosa and Cuscus hills, Dourada's foothills. I soon arrived at the Gomes Stream, near a farm house. The bridge was new and its heads, recently grounded, were soft clay. I sank until the middle of my ankles. A young man, watching me pass by, shouted from the house balcony: “You will get bogged down!” I took advantage of the communication establishment to ask where the path would be. He indicated the direction with his arm. I left the clay area, passed through the middle of the houses until I bordered the corral and left the farm.

There are several springs in this area, which flow from the *Cuscus* Hills and the Dourada Hills, forming the Cabra Stream, the Capão Stream and others.

Before crossing the Cabra Stream, I started hearing someone talking. I thought there was a house nearby, but I didn’t see anything, until, on a curve, I spotted a rural cellular phone antenna fixed on top of a small pole, with a tiny side cover attached to the pole, where a man could hardly stand. When I got to the antenna, there was the owner of the voice I had been listening, with a cell phone in his hand, sheltered in the small cover, talking carefree.

I arrived at a gate. I took the phone out of the backpack, which came all the way into a plastic bag, protected from humidity.

> *“Eu sou o caule dessas trepadeiras sem classe, nascidas na frincha das pedras. Bravias. Renitentes. Indomáveis. Cortadas.*

> *Maltratadas. Pisadas. E renascendo."* Cora Coralina

> *"I am the stem of these classless creepers, born in the stones crevice. Wild. Tough. Indomitable. Cut. Mistreated. Stepped. And reborning."* Cora Coralina

The land was getting steeper and wilder. I passed the Cabra Stream and the Vendinha Stream. There is a lot of loose gravel next to Vendinha. Apparently, the place must've been a mine. I passed by the water. There is no bridge or ford. You have to jump the small stream. There are pastures on the other side of the valley. The road passes directly above, where I went.

At 64 kilometers, I found another difference between the tracklog and the yellow footprints way. At a fork, the tracklog moved on straight ahead, but the footprints went to the right, entering the road that crossed the forest. I followed the footsteps. The woods were small. Soon after there were some ranch houses. I went through some wire gates and went up the path. I passed near the Vendinha's springs.

Suddenly, the footprints disappeared. I had passed in front of a deep and narrow passage, covered with trees, ground lined with protruding stones. I went back a little and saw yellow signs coming into it. It was a few meters into this ditch, maybe fifty, but it was the most sinister passage of the whole trip.

Leaving the ditch, a little more trail through the *cerrado* of the hill and I reached the highest point of the day, at 865 meters high. There, began a difficult section. It was not a slope, on the contrary, but I passed a dozen fences without gates and without the possibility of going under. At the first one, a new and high fence, I took out the panniers to jump. I put the load back, pedaled a little more and then another fence appeared. I realized that there would be many of them. I found a way of jumping without removing the panniers. It was the part of the trip that I made the most effort. Blessed bodybuilding! If it wasn't for it, I think I would not be strong enough to pass the bike over so many fences.

I went around the steep west edge of this hill, taking singletrack trails, until I found the way down, which entered pastures. This section has little defined trails. Yellow markings are painted on stones and trees. It is necessary to pay close attention. It is almost like navigating by azimuth.

I followed the tributaries of the Praia Stream (Beach Stream), crossing sections of riparian forest. When I got to the Praia Stream, I lost the track of Cora. I realized it soon, and went back to the last sign I had seen, where I found the trail again. The path enters the stream wood, so, when I passed, I didn't notice the footprints entering the forest. The riparian forest was flooded, it even looked like a bog. I believe it was so because of the recent rains. Despite this, the ground was firm, I didn't pick up much clay. I crossed the stream and left the woods. I followed trails in the pasture for five hundred meters following the stream, until crossing it again, this time by ford. I washed the bike by taking out the clay that had stuck in it when a passed the woods.

Following the path, I passed a new concrete bridge over a stream whose name I do not know, and, at 68 kilometers, when I reached a dirt road, I found the abandoned tracklog path again.

I started making stops each ten kilometers. In each stop, I rested for some minutes and drank some Gatorade.

A few more kilometers and I saw, on the right side of the road, some ruins. They were walls of red clay bordering a grove. A plaque explains what that place is: the ruins are what remains of the Ouro Fino's Our Lady of Pilar Church and the adjacent cemetery.

> *"Todos estamos matriculados na escola da vida, onde o mestre é o tempo."* Cora Coralina

> *"We are all enrolled in the school of life, where the master is time."* Cora Coralina

Ouro Fino (Thin Gold)

Village founded in 1727 by Bartolomeu Bueno da Silva (son), a *bandeirante* who became known as Second Anhanguera, who mined alluvial gold in the Praia Stream. As the gold extracted was powdered, the place gained the name of Ouro Fino (Thin Gold).

One of the tombs of the abandoned cemetery would be of Chico Mineiro, protagonist of history that became success of the country duo Tonico and Tinoco. According to the legend, this Ouro Fino would be the famous Ouro Fino of the country classic "Chico Mineiro". The authors of the song were the singer Tonico (João Salvador Pérez) and Francisco Ribeiro, who was a concierge of a radio based in São Paulo city, frequented by the famous duo. The song would have originated when the then concierge Francisco presented a poem on a radio show, reminding Tonico of the story told by his father when he was a child. Based on the poem and its memories, the lyrics were written. The song tells the story of two friends who only discover themselves brothers when one of them, Chico Mineiro, dies at a party in Ouro Fino. The oral tradition of Goiás states that such a story is true, that Chico Mineiro would be a cattle buyer, who was killed in Ouro Fino and buried there.

In the mid-twentieth century, with the move of the Capital of Goiás to Goiânia and the fall of a bridge, the village was abandoned. The once thriving village had a church, cemetery, houses of commerce, housing and even a seminar.

What remains of Ouro Fino goes unnoticed to road users, but the area is demarcated, being considered an archaeological site by IPHAN since 1996.

- - -

The road got busier. There were several houses near the road. Some horse riders passed me. I found guans and toucans through the woods I crossed, and also many loose animals, oxen and horses, grazing on the abundant grass of the road sides.

> *"Eu sou a fonte original de toda vida. Sou o chão que se prende à tua casa. Sou a telha da coberta de teu lar. A mina constante de teu poço. Sou a espiga generosa de teu gado e certeza tranquila ao teu esforço. Sou a razão de tua vida. De mim vieste pela mão do Criador, e a mim tu voltarás no fim da lida. Só em mim acharás descanso e Paz. Eu sou a grande Mãe universal. Tua filha, tua noiva e desposada. A mulher e o ventre que fecundas. Sou a gleba, a gestação, eu sou o amor."* Cora Coralina

> *"I'm the original source of all life. I'm the ground that attaches to your house. I am the tile of the roofing of your home. The constant spring of*

> *your well. I am the generous corn ear of your cattle and quiet certainty to your effort. I'm the reason of your life. From me you came by the hand of the Creator, and to me you will return at the end of the deal. Only in me will you find rest and Peace. I am the great universal Mother. Your daughter, your bride and wife. The woman and the womb that you fertilize. I'm the glebe, the gestation, I'm the love."* Cora Coralina

I found four cowboys leaving pasture area. They were accompanied by pack of Australian cattle dogs. There were seven dogs. They drank water in a puddle when I approached and I wasn't noticed. Before I got too close, I braked the rear brake to make noise and alert them. Then, they saw me. The most daring came running towards me, barking, and was soon accompanied by his partners. I stopped. Fortunately, the cowboys shouted at the dogs that calmed down, smelled the pannier, the bike, my feet and legs. That was all, they didn't attack me.

I arrived at the valley of the Vermelho River (Red River), important in national history. The City of Goiás was born on its banks, the Cora Coralina's House lays down on its banks. Vermelho River floods have destroyed the city a few times.

To the north were the headwaters of the Vermelho River and to the south was the beautiful São Francisco Hills, buttress of the Dourada Hills that goes northwest. Mountain range full of forest, the City of Goiás is at your feet.

I passed by the Vai-Vem Stream bridge. Rumor has it that it was a haunted bridge. The horses flinched, became uncontrollable, indocile, refused to pass by the bridge, doing so only forced. The animals that did not fall from the bridge arrived exhausted at the other side, useless to continue journey. My bike also flinched while slipping on the accumulated sand over the bridge, but I passed unharmed.

> *"De todos os tempos. De todos os povos. De todas as latitudes. Ela vem do fundo imemorial das idades e carrega a carga pesada dos mais torpes sinônimos, apelidos e apodos: Mulher da zona, Mulher da rua, Mulher perdida, Mulher à-toa. Mulher da vida, minha irmã. Pisadas, espezinhadas, ameaçadas. Desprotegidas e exploradas. Ignoradas da Lei, da Justiça e do Direito."* Cora Coralina

> *"Of all time. Of all peoples. Of all latitudes. She comes from the immemorial background of ages and carries the heavy load of the vilest synonyms, nicknames and sobriquets: Whore, Streetwalker, Strumpet, Courtesan. Whore, my sister. Stepped, trampled, threatened. Unprotected and exploited. Ignored by Legislation, Justice and Law."* Cora Coralina

One kilometer and a half later, I came across a long wall to the left of the road and a beautiful white colonial church with green details. I arrived in Ferreiro (Blacksmith).

Ferreiro (Blacksmith)

Ferreiro Village was born around 1727, being contemporary to Ouro Fino Village and Santana Village (Old Goiás). There lived an artisan, master in the smithy, a blacksmith, hence the name of the place. With the depletion of mines, the activity of the village migrated to agriculture, which disaggregated the urban nucleus giving rise to farms and ranches.

São João Batista Church (Saint John the Baptist Church)

The São João Batista Church was built in 1761. It is a simple temple, single nave, two-water swallow-like roof. The chancel has a wooden plank altar. Above the entrance door, there is a choir and an oculus window at the top of the facade, which illuminates the interior. Its walls are made of pylon mud and adobe, and the floor is made of *mezanela*. There is a small bell suspending on beams on the outside, on the right.

Next to it, there's a cemetery and, adjacent to the church, auxiliary side rooms were built. It was listed by IPHAN in 1953. In 2012, the chapel was restored.

\- - -

The stop was quick. The main door of the church was open. When I opened it, some birds flew away. I had a fright but I entered. The church remains well preserved, despite the slightly dirty walls.

Following the path, I passed the Prisca Stream and soon reached the GO-164 Highway. On the other side of the road was a large yellow arrow attached to a tree indicating left.

It was very little left to finish my cycle trip and one of the most awaited parts for me was coming: the passage through the Royal Road in the Imperial Road Natural Municipal Park. I went down the road in no hurry, enjoying the landscape of the park cut by the highway. Suddenly, I got out the tracklog, but I did not see the Cora's footprints indicating deviation. I came back a little and the tracklog indicated a narrow road, abandoned, being taken by the bush, where there was a well-closed gate with thick chain and big padlock. I was in doubt: did I miss any footprint? I continued down paved road, but besides not appearing the yellow signs, I was very close to the city. I decided to go back to the last mark I had passed. I returned. I climbed the highway until the dirt road exit. I turned the bike and returned very attentive, but it happened the same: the marks are gone and the tracklog entered the gate. I tried to get information in a restaurant, but even though it was open, there was no one there. I shouted: “Is anybody here?” But no one came. Was it a haunted restaurant? I had to follow the highway.

It did not take me long to get to the city entrance. I arrived in the City of Goiás! Instead of going straight to the city center, I went to Largo da Carioca (Carioca Square), where the Royal Road reached the city. I crossed the Vermelho River and retook the path. I slowly crossed the city streets that took me downtown, observing the beautiful colonial houses architecture. I passed the Rosary Church and, at 4 p.m., I reached the end point, the Bridge’s Old House, the Cora Coralina’s House, the end of my pilgrimage through the inland Goiás.

Day summary: 91 kilometers traveled with 1,336 meters of ascent.

I crossed the Vermelho River by the Lapa Bridge. In the small square in front of the bridge is the Anhanguera’s Cross, fixed on square platform four meters high, built over four columns.

> *“Rio Vermelho - meu rio. Rio que atravessei um dia (Altas horas. Mortas horas.) há cem anos… Em busca do meu destino.”* Cora Coralina

> *"Red River - my river. River that I crossed one day (High hours. Dead hours.) a hundred years ago… In search of my destiny."* Cora Coralina

Beside the bridge, men of the city sold *cerrado* fruits. *Pequi* and *mangaba* bowls stood out on the parapet that accompanies the river in the urban area. I checked the fruits. I tried the ripe *mangabas* (delicious!) and I promised to stop when I left town to buy a bowl.

It was the sellers who indicated good and cheap inns in the city. I chose Pousada do Sol (Sun Inn). Well located, fair price and the best: bike friendly! I was able to wash the bike and equipment on the lawn next to the parking lot and leave it outside the room without any hassle.

After a bath, I went to walk through downtown and appreciate the city architecture. Goiás has a huge and well-maintained historical center. There are several museums and churches. The houses preserve their 18th-century facades, taking us on a journey through time.

My dinner was at Ouro Fino Pizza. I do not usually drink alcohol, but I ordered a beer to celebrate the completion of the trip. I chose a dark beer, long neck. I was drinking it slowly, but on an empty stomach. I realized I was getting a little high. I checked the alcoholic graduation: 11%. That is why it went up fast. The alcohol effect hadn't passed even after eating the pizza. I do not know how I got back to the hotel, but I slept great!

X

Goiás

City of Goiás, October 20, 2018.

***"Goiás, minha cidade... Eu sou aquela amorosa de tuas ruas estreitas, curtas, indecisas, entrando, saindo uma das outras. Eu sou aquela menina feia da ponte da Lapa. Eu sou Aninha."* Cora Coralina**

"Goiás, my city... I am that loving one of its narrow, short, undecided streets, coming in, coming out of each other. I am that ugly girl from Lapa bridge. I am Aninha." Cora Coralina

It is like the song says: *"Quando eu quero mais, eu vou pra 'Goiais'!"* (When I want more, I go to Goiás!) It's beautiful, there is no denying it. The State of Goiás is one of the most beautiful Brazilian states. Its natural and historical characteristics are uniques.

The name Goiás is of indigenous origin. The Goiá nation inhabited large tracts of land in Central Brazil. Goiá or Guoyá comes from the Tupi and means "people of the same race".

Cidade de Goiás (City of Goiás)

In 1683, the *bandeirante* Bartolomeu Bueno da Silva arrived at the headwaters of the Vermelho River, in the Dourada Hills. Seeing Indians women adorned with gold pieces, he asked where the metal came from, but the natives did not want to reveal the source. To force them, he filled a plate of *cachaça* (sugarcane liquor), set it on fire, and told the natives that he would set the rivers on fire if they didn't show him where the gold would be. The Indians were impressed and started to call the *bandeirante* of Anhanguera, which means "devil-who-was", "diabolical" or "old devil". Bartolomeu returned to São Paulo carrying gold and captive Indians.

In 1722, the *bandeira* of Anhanguera's son departs from São Paulo, who, having the same name as his father, Bartolomeu Bueno da Silva, earned the same nickname. The *bandeira* roamed the Brazilian Highlands for four years, until finally finding the place where Anhanguera-Father had planted swidden. On the place, in 1726, Anhanguera-Son founded Arraial da Barra, present-day Buenolândia, and the following year founded the villages of Ouro Fino, Ferreiro and Santana.

In 1739, the municipality was created, and Santana Village was named Villa Boa de Goyaz (Good Village of Goyaz), in honor of its founder, with “Boa” derived from “Bueno”. In 1818, Vila Boa became the administrative headquarters of the Captaincy of Goiás and the name of the city became only Goiás. Until 1937, the City of Goiás was the State Capital, when the decree that transferred the Capital to Goiânia was signed.

- - -

Walking through the City of Goiás is like going back to the past. If it weren’t for the cars, the poles, the power lines, the modern clothes of passersby, in certain corners of the city we would see the same landscape as the 18th century. There are many historic buildings, museums, churches. The City of Goiás retains about 90% of its 18th-century architecture. In 2001, it received the title of Historical and Cultural Heritage of Humanity from UNESCO.

Those who arrive in Goiás by the Way of Cora Coralina have the first contact with the beautiful colonial architecture in the streets Dom Bosco, Luiz Guedes Amorim and Dom Cândido. At the end of the latter, on the banks of the Vermelho River, is the beautiful Bridge Old House, the Cora Coralina’s House. Worth the visit. We know not only the history of Cora but also the architecture of the house and its most interesting details.

Crossing the Lapa Bridge over the Vermelho River, just ahead, is the Anhanguera's Cross.

Cruz do Anhanguera (Anhanguera's Cross)

On the small square in front of the bridge, place where the Lapa Church existed, destroyed by flooding in the 19th century, is fixed the Anhanguera's Cross on a square platform with four meters high, built over four thick concrete columns. A metal plate fixed to the base provides information about it:

> "Cruz do Anhanguera. Descoberta em 1915 pelo Dr. Luiz Ramos de Oliveira Couto. Implantada em 17 de setembro de 1918."

> "Anhanguera's Cross. Discovered in 1915 by Dr. Luiz Ramos de Oliveira Couto. Installed on September 17, 1918."

The cross that has been there since 2002 is not the original one. On the last day of 2001, a violent flood in the Vermelho River took the original cross with it, which was found two days later buried in the mud. The cross, in pieces, didn't return to the square. A replica was placed in its place. The original cross was taken to the *Bandeiras* Museum, where it is exhibited.

Anhanguera's Cross was found in 1915, in Catalão, city in southeastern Goiás. It was settled near farm house, on the banks of the Ouvidor Stream, about six kilometers from the old Porto Velho do Rio

Paranaíba. The cross was fixed beside the oldest access trail to Goiás, opened by the Anhanguera-Son's *bandeira*. When the flag passed through there, one of the priests stood at the site to plant swiddens. This priest was originally from Catalonia, that is, he was Catalan, from which the name of the city was derived.

Discovered by Luiz Couto, at the base of the cross there was the inscription "172", being the last number unreadable. Couto considered to be "2" the missing number, which would confirm to be the cross left as a landmark by the Anhanguera's *bandeira*. The cross was then transported to Catalan and later to the City of Goiás.

There is no way to state categorically that the cross that is in the Bandeiras Museum is actually the cross left by the Anhanguera-Son's *bandeira*, but there are strong indications, such as the place where it was found and the date inscribed on the base. In addition, the *bandeirantes* used to fix crosses in the localities where they passed to "mark territory".

\- - -

My wife would arrive in town only in the afternoon. She was driving from Brasilia. With the morning free, I went to walk around the city, to know its museums. My first destination was the Paulo Bertran Memorial. I walked from the downtown to the institute's head office, at Dona Sinhá Inn. I was welcomed by Irene, who kindly opened the doors of the place.

Paulo Bertran Memorial

Paulo Bertran Wirth Chaibub was born in Anápolis in 1948. He graduated in Economics from the University of Brasilia and specialized in History at the University of Strasbourg (France).

A few years ago, I came across the book *História da Terra e do Homem no Planalto Central (History of Land and Man in the Brazilian Highlands)*, by Paulo Bertran. I became a fan of the author. Like most Brazilians, I imagined that the history of the Federal District had begun when president Juscelino Kubitschek decided to move the Capital to the Brazilian Highlands, but after moving to Brasilia, I found that around here there was a lot more history than I thought. The book totally changed my view on what the Brazilian Highlands was before JK, before Luís Cruls walked these *sertões* to define the area where Brasilia would one day be built, even before the pioneers raided these lands.

For those who like history and want to get to know the Brazilian Highlands better, it is a must-read book. In eighteen chapters, Bertran recounts legends and myths, enumerates *bandeirantes* and scientists who have traveled through Brazilian hinterland, details the gold exploration, characterizes *Homo cerratensis*, describes the economy of the old cities, lists famous places and some that are present in historical documents, but that were never found.

In 2003, Paulo and some friends created the Bertran Fleury Institute in Brasilia. After his death, the institute gained its own headquarters in the City of Goiás. Thus was born the Paulo Bertran Memorial, a museum that holds part of his library, some of his belongings, objects, statues, etc.

Bertran died in Goiânia in 2005 at the age of 56, leaving as a legacy works of great value.

- - -

I couldn't talk to Paulo's widow, Maria das Graças Fleury Curado, who lives in Goiânia.

I went back to downtown. I went to see the museums. The first visit was to the home of my traveling companion, Cora Coralina.

The Cora Coralina's House Museum is located in the house where Cora Coralina lived at different times of her life: in childhood and youth, with parents; and when she returned to Goiás, already a widow. The building belongs to the Brazilian Federal Government, purchased from the family for a symbolic price. The museum houses photos, manuscripts, household items, furniture and books, collection belonging to the heirs. The guided tour helps to understand the story of the confectioner-writer and get to know inside the architecture of colonial houses of Goiás. The house was built around 1770 and had several residents before being bought by Cora's great-great-grandfather, Sergeant-Major João José do Couto Guimarães. It is a huge house of sixteen rooms, large backyard and drinking water fountain.

> *"Minha Casa Velha da Ponte... assim a vejo e conto, sem datas e sem assentos."* Cora Coralina

> *"My Bridge Old House... thus I see it and tell, without dates and without seats."* Cora Coralina

After the visit to Cora's house, I went to the Palácio do Conde dos Arcos (Count of the Arches Palace), which was the Goiás Government seat until the Capital was transferred to Goiânia. It was named after the first governor of the then Captaincy of Goiás, Dom Marcos de Noronha, the Count of Arches. The palace was built in the 18th century and underwent several renovations. The collection consists of furniture and objects from various eras.

State decree determines that the State Capital be temporarily transferred to the City of Goiás once a year, on its anniversary day (July 25), when the Palace of the Count of Arcos is once again the government seat.

From there I went to the Bandeiras Museum, which is housed in a mansion built also in the 18th century to be a chamber and prison house. On the ground floor was the jail, whose access was only by trapdoors on the first floor. There were no doors on the ground floor. The first floor was accessible by wooden stairs on the outside of the building. The large halls of the first floor served the legislative and judicial powers of that time. What draws the most attention: the Anhanguera's Cross; the utensils and tools used in mining and goldsmithing; and the jails, huge, with wide walls of pylon mud.

- - -

My wife arrived at noon. We strolled around the city, had lunch at the Braseiro Restaurant, typical Goian food, on Senador Caiado Street, at the beginning of the square where the Chafariz da Boa Morte (Good Death Fountain) is. In addition to the good food, the restaurant has *cerrado* fruit juices.

The city is very quiet. During Saturday night there was little movement through the streets. We had dinner downtown: empadão goiano (Goian pie).

XI

Final

City of Goiás, October 21, 2018.

We had breakfast and left back to Brasilia. Before leaving town, I passed the Lapa Bridge where the fruit vendors were. As I promised, I bought two bowls of *mangaba*. Some of them were very large, they looked like peaches, but the tip is: the smallest are the tastiest.

Time to go home. Time to think about this lonely journey. It's good to spend some time alone, suffering on the bicycle. Every little pleasure is valued. The hot water in the bottle, the smashed withered bread sandwich, the thin shadow of the *cerrado* trees, the freshness of the streams, the warmth of the sun, the solidarity of the human being, the smiles, the people's looks and inquiries. Moment of valuing what we have at home and goes unnoticed in daily life: food, comfort, family, work.

Thanks, my God, for our health. Thank you, family, for your support. Thanks, bicycle, for always taking me through life. Thank you, Cora Coralina, by the words of encouragement left on the way plates.

> ***"O que vale na vida não é o ponto de partida e sim a caminhada. Caminhando e semeando, no fim, terás o que colher."*** **Cora Coralina**

> *"What is worth in life is not the starting point, but the walk. Walking and sowing, in the end, you will have what to reap."* Cora Coralina

Did you enjoy the trip? Do it you too.

If you liked what you read and were interested in making the same trip, follow this link: https://serpedalante.com/cora . You can see photos, maps, and download tracklogs and trip planning worksheets.

I would like to know your opinion about this book. Leave your message in the blog comments.

References

1. Bertran, Paulo. História da Terra e do Homem no Planalto Central: ECO-HISTÓRIA DO DISTRITO FEDERAL - Do Indígena ao Colonizador. 2nd edition. Brasília: UNB, 2011.

2. Way of Cora Coralina's website. Available at: <http://www.caminhodecoracoralina.com.br>. Access at: January 11, 2019.

3. Cora Coralina Museum website. Available at: <http://www.museucoracoralina.com.br>. Access at: January 11, 2019.

4. DM blog. A Cruz do Anhanguera. Available at: <http://www.dm.com.br/entretenimento/2018/05/a-cruz-do-anhanguera.html>. Access at: February 11, 2019.

5. Morais, Lucinete Aparecida. Comunidade do Ferreiro (GO): a terra, a luta e o sagrado. 2017. 106. Postgraduate essay - Universidade Federal de Goiás, Goiânia, 2015.

6. Melo, Laura Ludovico de. Ouro Fino: Um arraial ... uma igreja ... um largo ... e uma vaga lembrança na paisagem. 2014. 20. Manuscript - Pontifícia Universidade Católica de Goiás. 2014.

7. Website of the Municipality of Santo Antônio do Descoberto. Available at: <https://santoantoniododescoberto.go.gov.br/novo/index.php/historia/historico>. Access at: February 12, 2019.

8. Curta Mais website. Available at: <http://curtamais.com.br/goiania/olhos-dagua-a-cidade-do-interior-de-goias-no-meio-do-caminho-de-goiania-a-brasilia-que-encantou-carlos-drummond-de-andrade>. Access at: February 12, 2019.

9. Olhos d'Água website. Available at: <http://ricardojsabino.wixsite.com/olhosdagua/historia>. Access at: February 12, 2019.

10. IBGE website. Available at: <https://biblioteca.ibge.gov.br/visualizacao/dtbs/goias/corumbadegoias.pdf>. Access at: February 12, 2019.

11. Pirenópolis City Hall website. Available at: <https://www.pirenopolis.go.gov.br/municipio/a-cidade>. Access at: February 14, 2019.

12. Website of the Parish of Our Lady of the Rosary of Pirenópolis. Available at: <http://www.paroquiadorosario.org.br/portal/institucional/nossa-hostoria>. Access at: February 15, 2019.

13. Babylon Farm website. Available at: <http://www.fazendababilonia.com.br/historia>. Access at: January 15, 2019.

14. Website of the Municipality of São Francisco de Goiás. Available at: <http://saofranciscodegoias.go.gov.br/pagina/185--historia-da-cidade>. Access at: January 20, 2019.

15. GOIÁS. ACT #18,844, JUNE 10, 2015. Changes the name and delimits the area of the Jaraguá Hills State Park and provides other arrangements, Goiânia, GO. Available at: <http://www.gabinetecivil.goias.gov.br/leis_ordinarias/2015/lei_18844.htm>. Access at: February 16, 2019.

16. iPatrimônio website. Available at: <http://www.ipatrimonio.org/?p=19659>. Access at: January 15, 2019.

17. IBGE website. Available at: <https://cidades.ibge.gov.br/brasil/go/jaragua/historico>. Access at: January 17, 2019.

18. Website of the Municipality of Jaraguá. Available at: <http://www.jaragua.go.gov.br/pagina/202-historia->. Access at: January 18, 2019.

19. Jaraguá City website. Available at: <http://www.jaraguago.com.br/historia.php>. Access at: January 18, 2019.

20. iPatrimônio website. Available at: <http://www.ipatrimonio.org/?p=49244>. Access at: January 18, 2019.

21. Itaguari City Hall website. Available at: <https://www.itaguari.go.gov.br/sobre-o-municipio/historia/>. Access at: January 18, 2019.

22. Receptivo Araraúna website. Available at: <http://caminhodecora.tur.br/mountainbike/175km-sao-francisco-goias>. Access at: January 19, 2019.

23. Mugnaini JR., Ayrton. Enciclopédia das Músicas Sertanejas. 1st edition. São Paulo: Letras & Letras, 2001.

24. Bertran Fleury Institute website. Available at: <http://institutobertranfleury.org.br>. Access at: February 2, 2019.

The author

Evandro Torezan was born in Londrina, State of Paraná. He lives in Brasilia since 2008. Graduated in Computer Science from the State University of Londrina. Public employee since 2009, in 2012, joined the Federal Court of Accounts (Tribunal de Contas da União). Passionate about cycling, always wrote about it, reporting his adventures on the blog Ser Pedalante (serpedalante.com). In 2017, he published his first book, *De catedral a catedral* (From cathedral to cathedral), where he recounts his struggle to became a Brazilian public employee.

Get to know the author's other books. Follow the link https://serpedalante.com/livros .

www.ingramcontent.com/pod-product-compliance
Ingram Content Group UK Ltd.
Pitfield, Milton Keynes, MK11 3LW, UK
UKHW041957190726
13854UKWH00005B/2019